Skyline 4

Student's Book

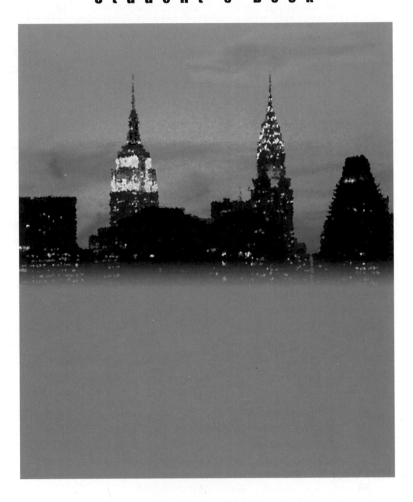

Simon Brewster

Paul Davies

Mickey Rogers

MACMILLAN

Contents

Functions	Vocabulary	Pronunciation
• Making polite requests for information • Talking about causes and effects / situations and decisions • Reporting other people's ideas	• Compound and paired words • Expressions related to the home • Adjectives to describe character	• Rhythm
• Talking about processes / past events • Defining what / who you're talking about	• Words / expressions related to jobs • Financial	• Word stress
• Confirming / questioning information	• Appliances / technology • Environment • Cars	• Contrastive stress • Intonation – question tags
• Talking about setting up / carrying out projects • Talking about habits and states in the past	• Multi-word verbs • Describing interiors	• Intonation – questions
• Talking about background facts / past circumstances • Talking about previous events	• Crime • Law	• Past tense forms
• Reporting what people have said, opinions they have given • Debating points	• Nouns as adjectives • Reporting verbs • Expressions for discussions	• Word stress

Contents

Songsheets

Functions	Vocabulary	Pronunciation
• Describing people / places / things / events	• Clothing • Shopping items • Music / instruments	• Linking
• Talking about obligation and necessity • Indicating time	• Weddings and graduations • Inviting	• Intonation – showing interest
• Talking about past conditions / cause and effect • Expressing regret	• Gender • Practical / ethical issues • Discussion	• Sentence stress – conditionals
• Speculating about past events / actions	• Experiential • Historical	• Weak forms – modals
• Talking about future events	• People: from cradle to grave • Linking words	• Linking
• Getting ideas across clearly • Analyzing / discussing language	• Language of prediction • Computer words and expressions	• Intonation and emotion

Unit 1 Relationships and communication

1 Parents and children

1 Speaking and listening

a What do you think is happening in each photograph below?

b Listen to three pieces of conversation. Match each with the appropriate photograph.

1 ....   2 ....   3 ....

c In groups, discuss the following question.

What topics do parents talk about with their 15–16 year-old children?

2 Listening and speaking

a Listen to Claudia, 15, and her mother talking. Check (✔) the topics you hear.

money ◯	time on the phone ◯	messy bedroom ◯
school grades ◯	watching TV ◯	getting home late ◯
taking care of pets ◯	volume of stereo ◯	homework ◯

b Try to complete the following four house rules for Claudia. Listen to the conversation again and check.

1 No .... if the volume is too high.
2 No allowance money if she doesn't ....
3 No TV before she ....
4 No phone calls longer than ....

3 Grammar builder: review of past tenses and present perfect

a **Look at sentences 1–3. Match them to sentences a–c.**

1 I was cleaning my room.   a) Look how clean it is. I've done it three times this week.

2 I've cleaned my room.   b) Well ... uh ... last week.

3 I cleaned my room.   c) You called me, so I stopped.

b **Complete the following text with appropriate forms of the verbs in parentheses.**

Claudia (1) .... (*attend*) her present school for three years. Last year she (2) .... (*be*) first in her class in French. She (3) .... (*visit*) the French-speaking part of Canada three times. Her French (4) .... (*improve*) a lot while she (5) .... (*stay*) there with a family last summer. She (6) .... (*read*) several books in French since then too.

4 Pronunciation: rhythm

a **Listen to these sentences from the conversation between Claudia and her mother, and notice the rhythm. Underline the stressed syllables, as in sentence 1.**

1 I've turned it down.   4 Have you done your homework?

2 Look at the state of your room!   5 Susan went out with Jimmy?

3 I was cleaning my room when you called me.

b **Practice saying the sentences with the same rhythm.**

5 Speaking, reading and writing

a **In groups, make a list of ways to be a good, effective parent.**

Talk to your children about things that interest them.

Be consistent.

b **Read this extract from a pamphlet about ways to be an effective parent. How many of these ideas did you include in your list in exercise a?**

3 **Set rules and be consistent**
Discipline is necessary in every family. It can help children to behave acceptably and learn self-control. House rules might include no rudeness, no hitting and no TV until homework is done. Always follow through with consequences when rules are broken.

4 **Make time for your children**
There are fewer opportunities today for parents to be with their children. Do your best to be· available when your children, including older teens, want to talk or participate in family activities. Attend concerts, sports events, etc. with your teens – if they like you to!

5 **Make communication a priority**
Children want and deserve explanations of their parents' decisions and behavior. If you don't take time to explain, they will not appreciate your values and motives. Discuss problems with older children openly and find solutions together. When children participate in decisions they are much more likely to carry them out.

c **Write a short account of something that happened between you and your parents, or one of your parents, when you were in your teens. Exchange your compositions in pairs and discuss them.**

2 In the workplace

1 Speaking and reading

a In pairs or groups, discuss these questions.

1 What do you consider the main advantages of e-mail?

2 Do you think there are any disadvantages?

b Now read the article on the right and compare your ideas with it.

c Read the text again and list the positive and negative aspects of e-mail.

Positive	Negative

YOU'VE GOT MAIL

For many people today it's difficult to remember what life was like without e-mail. It has transformed communication at every level. It's cheap, quick, versatile and easy to use. An e-mail to Australia costs the same as a local phone call. You can attach documents and photographs. With a laptop computer, you can travel with your "office," and read or send e-mails any place you can access a telephone line.

You can use e-mail to communicate within a company as well as with suppliers and customers at other locations, including those in other countries. Young people communicate with friends by e-mail, and send each other e-mail greeting cards. When traveling, many people look for an Internet café, not a post office. In 1999, on an average day in the United States, 3.5 billion e-mail messages were sent. Before 2005, that figure will exceed 10 billion.

But there is a downside. Hardly anyone writes letters anymore, and many e-mails are very badly written, and often quite unnecessary. Also, e-mails can follow you wherever you go with a laptop so there's no escape from work. And e-mails accumulate rapidly – you may return after a vacation and find hundreds of e-mails waiting for you.

d Ask four or five other people whether they write or receive many of the following.

- personal letters
- business letters
- personal e-mails
- business e-mails

In groups, compare the results of your informal survey.

2 Word builder: compound and paired words

Form as many compounds / pairs as you can with one word from box A and another from box B.

bedroom

A

bed   down   greeting
home   house   Internet
laptop   telephone   post
school   self   work

B

room   café   call   cards
control   computer
grades   line   office
place   side   work

Learning tip

The compounding of nouns (e.g. *bedroom* and *bus station*, **not** *room for sleep* or *station of buses*) is typical of the English language. A major aspect of successful language learning is noticing such typical patterns. Can you think of some more examples that are different in English and your language – or very similar?

3 Listening

a Listen to the conversation between two people in an office. What are the topics of each part?

Part 1: ....

Part 2: ....

Part 3: ....

b Read questions 1–5, below. Listen to the conversation again, and answer the questions.

1 Who has written a report for John West?

2 When does John want it?

3 What is John's new e-mail address?

4 What is happening at Monica's house tonight?

5 Who knows how to get to her house, Barbara or Peter?

4 Grammar builder: review of polite requests for information

a In the listening text, John and Barbara are fairly polite to each other. Look at the following requests for information. What part of each request makes it polite?

1 Do you know if John West wants it today?

2 Can you tell me what John's new e-mail address is?

3 Do you know where she lives?

b What do you notice about the word order of these questions?

c Change these direct requests into more polite ones.

1 Where's the cafeteria? ....

2 Is it open now? ....

3 What time do they close? ....

4 Can you open a charge account? ....

5 How much does lunch cost? ....

5 Speaking

a Imagine you are teachers or administrative staff here where you study English. Work in pairs. Student A knows the place well; student B is new and asks student A polite questions about things like these.

- Office / reception opening / closing times, and class starting / finishing times.
- Classes on Saturday morning / afternoon / etc.
- The Director / Administrator / Coordinator / etc.
- Library / self-access center / restaurant / etc.

B: *Can you tell me where the Director's office is?*
Do you know if there's a supermarket near here?

b Now change roles and ask some more questions.

9

3 Between friends

1 Speaking and listening

a What is the most important quality in a friend? In pairs, put the qualities below in order of importance.

fun, good company ◯   honest ◯   intelligent and talented ◯   loyal ◯

patient and understanding ◯   reliable ◯   same interests ◯   same values ◯

b Describe the people in the photographs below. Then listen to five people talking about their friends. Match each speaker to a photograph.

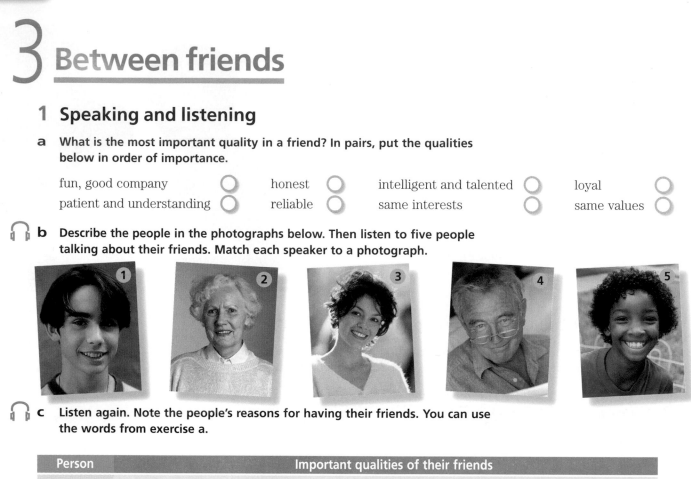

c Listen again. Note the people's reasons for having their friends. You can use the words from exercise a.

Person	Important qualities of their friends
1	
2	
3	
4	
5	

2 Reading and speaking

a Read and answer the following quiz. Then calculate your score, and read the interpretation of it.

ARE YOU A GOOD FRIEND?

1 If there were a great program on TV, and a close friend phoned sounding anxious to talk, would you:

a) make an excuse (e.g. that you were taking a shower), and say you would call back later?

b) forget the program and let your friend talk?

c) try to persuade your friend to come and watch the program?

2 Is the longest you have ever kept a close friend:

a) less than 1 year?

b) between 1 and 5 years?

c) more than 5 years?

3 If you were President, would you:

a) continue to see your present friends frequently?

b) forget your present friends completely in order to concentrate on your duties?

c) see your present friends one or two times a year, and send them Christmas cards?

4 When a close friend has trusted you with a personal secret, have you:

a) always kept the secret and never told anyone?

b) occasionally told the secret to another friend?

c) often told most of your other friends?

5 If you have a serious disagreement with a close friend, do you usually:

a) insist until the friend agrees with you or the friendship breaks down?

b) soon agree with your friend, or change the subject rather than let the problem grow?

c) drop the subject temporarily and try to understand your friend's point of view?

Scoring

1 a=5 b=15 c=10   2 a=5 b=10 c=15   3 a=15 b=5 c=10   4 a=15 b=10 c=5   5 a=5 b=10 c=15

Interpretation:

55–75 points – You consider friendship very important, and are good at making and keeping friends. You try hard to improve the relationships you have.

40–50 points – You consider friendship important, and are fairly good at making and keeping friends. However, you are not always as careful as you could be about maintaining good relations with friends.

25–35 points – You are probably a bit of a loner, and don't depend much on friends. However, if you do want friends, it is not difficult. If you are more sociable and help other people when you can, you will soon have friends.

b In pairs or groups, discuss your results in the quiz. Do they correspond to the facts? For example, are you a loner according to the quiz, but in fact you have many friends?

3 Grammar builder: zero, first and second conditionals

a In pairs, read sentences 1–3 below, and match them to sentences a–c.

1 If I have a disagreement with a friend, I change the subject.

2 You will make new friends if you join a sports club.

3 If I were President, I would not drop my present friends.

a) What you predict will happen as a result of a certain action.

b) What you would probably do in a hypothetical situation.

c) What you usually do in a specific situation.

b Complete the sentences with appropriate forms of the verbs in parentheses.

• Anne always (1) .... (*talk*) with her best friend if she (2) .... (*have*) a problem.

• If she (3) .... (*be*) free tomorrow, she (4) .... (*have*) lunch with some friends.

• If she (5) .... (*move*) to another part of the world, Anne (6) .... (*keep*) in contact with her friends.

4 Speaking

In groups, tell one another about your best friends in elementary school. What relationship do you have with them now?

LANGUAGE for life:
foreign *connections*

① Are you real users of English yet?

② Go on – try it!

Find out about your classmates, and let them find out about you! Conduct a survey using the form below. Put a check (✔) in the appropriate box for each person that answers YES or NO (there is no need for anyone's name).

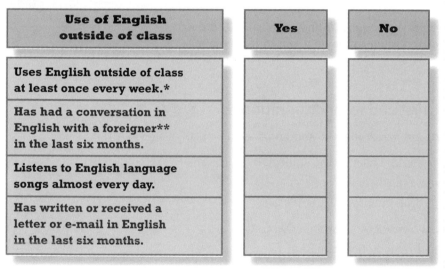

Use of English outside of class	Yes	No
Uses English outside of class at least once every week.*		
Has had a conversation in English with a foreigner** in the last six months.		
Listens to English language songs almost every day.		
Has written or received a letter or e-mail in English in the last six months.		

*Homework and study excluded – must be real communicative use of English

**English teachers excluded

Compare your results in groups, and discuss your findings.

- *How many of the people you surveyed answered YES in each category – none, a few, many, most, everyone?*
  How many answered NO in each category?
- *Are there any interesting cases in the class, or in this group – for example, someone with a foreign boy / girlfriend?*
- *How could you get more practice using English outside of class?*

At some point, students of English have to become users of English if they're really going to learn the language. For some people there's no choice and no problem – from early on they have to use the language regularly for study or work. But others don't, and they need to look for or create opportunities to use English outside of class. This is essential for progress beyond elementary level. If you are an intermediate level student of English who doesn't use English outside of class, it's time to change. It's time to become a real user!

One thing you can easily do is to read and listen to English. Anyone can find English language newspapers, magazines and even books to read, or music and videos to listen to and watch. As you practice your English, you can pursue your interests, and get a better idea of how foreigners view the world. You may disagree with some of those views, but it's better to know what others are up to in this global world!

The real problem is being able to interact with other people in English. But there are ways. Through Internet chat rooms you can now have "conversations" with people all over the world. There are still ways to establish traditional pen-pal relationships if you're a traditionalist. And in most places you can find at least a few foreigners who speak English (remember, it's not only Anglo-Saxons who speak English). If you really want to, you can use English.

③ Do you agree?

Discuss the text above in groups. Do you agree about how to progress beyond elementary level? What specific ideas are suggested in the text? What opportunities are there in your city or town to use English outside of class? Where can you:

- *get reading and listening materials?*
- *use e-mail or access chat rooms if you don't have a computer?*
- *meet foreigners?*

④ Action?

Why not plan to use English outside of class next week, and then compare your experiences?

⑤ Breaking the ice

It's not always easy to start a conversation with a stranger, foreign or not.
Listen to how some people do it, and note what they say.

1 ....
2 ....
3 ....
4 ....
5 ....

Why not practice opening – and continuing – conversations? If you all pretend to be interesting foreigners, it could be fun. (Of course, we're not suggesting that you're not interesting as yourself!)

Unit 2 Work and money

1 Working to live, or living to work?

1 Reading and speaking

a Read the two opinions below. Who works to live, and who lives to work?

"Work shouldn't dominate your life. Other interests and the time you spend with your family and friends are more important. My job's OK, but I'm not in any danger of becoming a workaholic."

"Work is central to life. If I didn't have a worthwhile and satisfying job, I'd be very depressed. In my experience, most people who aren't happy in their work aren't happy in life."

b Discuss these questions in pairs or groups.

1 Do you agree more with the woman or the man? Why?
2 How would you define the word *workaholic*?
3 Do you know any workaholics? Yourself, perhaps?

2 Listening and speaking

a Listen to Lisa and Jim talking about their jobs. What does each of them do?

b Look at the table. Listen to Lisa and Jim again. Complete the table putting plus (+) for each positive aspect of their jobs and minus (–) for each negative aspect.

	Lisa	Jim
1 salary	–	+
2 benefits (medical insurance, pension plan, etc.)		
3 nature of work		
4 working hours		
5 vacations		
6 training and development programs		
7 promotion opportunities		

c In groups, discuss the aspects of a job that are important to you. Look at the points in the table above, and suggest others, e.g. convenient location (near where you live), pleasant colleagues.

3 Word builder: vocabulary for talking about jobs

a   Complete this table of occupational vocabulary. Use a dictionary if you wish.
    Check in pairs.

Occupation "I'm a / an …"	Activity "I work in …"	Adjective "I'm in the … department."
1 ……………	accounts	accounting
administrator	administration	2 ……………
architect	3 ……………	architectural
4 ……………	chemistry	chemical
dentist	dentistry	5 ……………
doctor	6 ……………	medical
7 ……………	law	legal
manager	8 ……………	managerial
9 ……………	science	10 ……………

> **Language assistant**
> Nouns can often be used as adjectives, so you can say *chemistry department* and *law department* instead of chemical department and legal department.

b   Classify the following adjectives that can be used to describe jobs as
    normally positive (+), normally negative (–), or could be either (±).
    Check in pairs, using a dictionary when necessary.

boring	○	challenging	○	demanding	○
flexible	○	frustrating	○	interesting	○
satisfying	○	stressful	○	tiring	○
rewarding	○	varied	○	well-paid	○

4 Pronunciation: word stress

a   Listen to the following sets of words and underline the stressed syllables.

science scientist scientific   architecture architect architectural

b   Now say the following words and underline the stressed syllables.
    Then listen and check.

photography	psychology	management	chemistry
photographer	psychologist	manager	chemist
photographic	psychological	managerial	chemical

> **Learning tip**
> A good monolingual English dictionary is useful for expanding your understanding of vocabulary. In it, you can find:
> - the parts of speech a word can function as: *scientific* can only be an adjective, *scientist* only a noun, but *science* can be a noun (*I like science*) or an adjective (*a science book*);
> - the different meanings a word can have: *bore* as a verb can mean *to make people bored* (*The teacher bored us*) or to make a hole (*He bored through the wall*);
> - the connotations a word can have: *satisfactory* is neutral and *satisfying* is positive (*My job is satisfactory* vs. *My job is satisfying*).

5 Speaking

In pairs or groups, compare your own jobs and the jobs of people you know.
You may need vocabulary from the Word builder.

6 Writing

a   Write a paragraph about a job (e.g. administration), but DO NOT name the job.

In this job you have to …   You also …   It can be very …   The salary is usually …

b   Read your paragraph aloud to the class, and see if they can guess the job.

2 Winning and losing money

1 Word builder: financial vocabulary

a Match words 1–8 with a definition a–h.

1 gamble
2 capital
3 earn
4 profit
5 interest
6 invest
7 loss
8 win

a) money, usually calculated in percentages, earned by an investment
b) money earned by a business or investment, after deducting expenses
c) to make money from a competition or gambling
d) to risk money in a lottery or game, or to take risks in business, etc.
e) money lost in a business project or investment
f) to make money from work or investments
g) money you have that you can put into a business project or investment
h) to put money into a bank or company to earn interest

b Complete the sentences using the appropriate form of a word from the list above.

1 Enormous numbers of people .... every week in national lotteries, and a very small number .... a fortune.

2 The safest way to .... money is through a bank savings or deposit account, but the .... rates are usually low.

3 The basic idea of business is to invest .... and make a good ....

4 There is always an element of risk in business: instead of .... money, you may take a ...., and even go bankrupt.

2 Speaking and listening

a Look at the pictures. In pairs, discuss these questions.

1 What do the pictures represent?
2 Do you ever gamble in one of these ways, or in another way?

b Listen to a radio interview about gambling in Britain. Which of the three types of gambling in the pictures is the interview about?

c Answer the following questions. Listen to the interview again and check your answers. Compare your revised answers with other students.

1 What do ordinary people who win a fortune often do?
2 Why?
3 What is the most sensible thing to do?

d In groups, discuss these questions.

1   Do you know any people who have won a lot of money and then lost it again?

2   Have you ever won a large sum of money or a valuable prize?

3 Grammar builder: review of passive constructions

a Look at the following sentences, and underline the verb constructions as in the example.

1   Sometimes, millions of dollars <u>are won</u> by one person.

2   The fortune was lost again in a year or two.

3   A million dollars can be spent very quickly.

4   The money should be invested.

b In pairs, discuss this question.

Are there passive constructions like these in your language?

c Complete the paragraph below using the verbs in parentheses.

The Old Mill (1) .... (*build*) in 1895 by Caleb Fuller. The building (2) .... (*design*) as a textile factory, but later it (3) .... (*use*) as a hospital, a prison, and then a shopping mall. The Town Council is currently remodeling it for its new function, the Old Mill Museum and Cultural Center. The work should (4) .... (*complete*) within four months, and the Center will (5) .... (*inaugurate*) by the Mayor on September 23. The varied history of the Old Mill (6) .... (*record*) in a recently published book by Selma Brett-Howard, *If Buildings Could Speak.*

Language assistant

The passive is used to focus attention on the person or thing affected by an action, rather than on the doer of the action. Often, the doer is not known: *A Picasso painting* **was stolen** *last night.*

4 Speaking, writing and reading

a In groups, select an institution in your city or country (a bank, a manufacturing company, a college, etc.), and discuss what you know about its history from the time it was founded.

b Write a brief history of the institution. Look at the example in exercise 3c. Exchange your history with another group, and read their version.

3 Entrepreneurs

1 Speaking and reading

a In pairs, discuss the photographs, and the possible connections between them. What do you think is special about The Body Shop products?

b Read the article quickly, and see if your ideas about The Body Shop products were right.

c Read the text again and complete the information in the fact box.

NICE PEOPLE DO WIN

Anita Roddick, who founded The Body Shop, is one of the most successful entrepreneurs in the world. But she thinks that businesses should operate humanely and deal only in products which are environmentally friendly. There appear to be millions of women and men that agree with her.

In the many countries she visited as a young traveler, Anita Roddick noticed the natural substances the local women use to care for their skin and hair. She realized there was no need for the synthetic ingredients, cruel animal testing, and wasteful packaging that are used in the modern cosmetics industry.

The Body Shop, which produces and sells only natural skin and hair care products, first opened in England in 1976. There are now 1,500 stores in 47 countries. It has grown into a $1 billion business with 86 million customers. It was one of the first cosmetics companies that made products for men. Anita Roddick is a real businesswoman, but one who cares about the environment and social justice. She has shown that profit and ethics are not necessarily in conflict. She is an example other entrepreneurs should follow.

The Body Shop

Founded in (1) .... in (2) ....

Now a business worth (3) ...., with (4) .... stores in

(5) .... countries and (6) .... customers.

GUIDING PRINCIPLES	• All products are made from (7) .... ingredients.
	• No products are tested on (8) ....
	• No wasteful (9) ....

2 Grammar builder: review of relative clauses

a In pairs, look at the sentences below, especially the underlined sections. Then match 1–4 with a–d.

The Body Shop deals only in <u>products</u> <u>which</u> are environmentally friendly.

Anita Roddick is a <u>businesswoman</u> <u>who</u> cares about the environment and social justice.

There are millions of <u>women and men</u> <u>that</u> agree with Anita Roddick.

The Body Shop was <u>one of the first cosmetics companies</u> <u>that</u> made products for men.

The Body Shop employs <u>the natural substances</u> <u>the local women</u> use.

Anita Roddick is <u>an example</u> <u>other entrepreneurs</u> should follow.

1	"Which" is used	a)	after nouns referring to people
2	"Who" is used	b)	when another noun is the subject of the following verb
3	"That" is used	c)	after nouns referring to either people or things
4	"Which / who / that" can be omitted	d)	after nouns referring to things

b In pairs, write the following pairs of sentences as single sentences, with relative clauses. When possible, omit *which / who / that*. Compare your sentences with other students.

1 Anita Roddick is a businesswoman. She has made a fortune.
2 The Body Shop is a $1 billion company. Anita Roddick founded it.
3 The Body Shop sells skin and hair care products. They have entirely natural ingredients.
4 Anita Roddick has a philosophy. Millions of women and men share it.
5 Entrepreneurs are dynamic people. They establish new businesses, often innovative ones.
6 In Europe there are many historic cities. American tourists often visit them.

3 Speaking

a In groups, discuss what you know about the people and things in the pictures below.

b Now discuss the kind of people and events that you really like or hate.

Student 1	*I hate weddings that ...*	*The reason is that ...*	*How do you feel about weddings?*
Student 2	*I love people who ...*	*I suppose that's because ...*	*What about you?*
Student 3	*I love parties which ...*	*I always ...*	*What kind of parties do you like?*

19

LANGUAGE for life:
armchair *shopping*

① Home delivery

You're at home, feeling tired but hungry. There's nothing to eat in the kitchen. It's dark and raining outside. You can:

1 go to bed hungry.
2 go out to the nearest restaurant.
3 call for a pizza.

What would you usually do? Have you been in that situation? If so, what did you do?

Compare your answers in groups. Then discuss these questions.

- *Is there anyone in the group who regularly orders food by phone?*
- *Where from?*
- *Why?*
- *Is there anyone who never orders food by phone?*
- *Why not?*

② Magic plastic

Telephone ordering of food for home delivery is just one kind of armchair shopping. People usually pay cash for their pizza. But most other armchair shopping is paid for by check or, most often, credit card. Do you know the history of the credit card? No? Well, guess what's happening in the scene shown below. Have you ever been in a similar situation?

Now listen to a radio talk, and decide which part of the talk the picture is illustrating. Then listen again and note the following information.

1 Year when Frank McNamara decided to start Diners Club credit cards: ....

2 Number of cards issued by McNamara in the first year: ....

3 Number of restaurants that accepted that first Diners Club card: ....

4 Bank that issued the first widely used credit card: ....

5 Year that card was introduced: ....

6 Present name of that card: ....

7 Name another credit card that was introduced in 1958: ....

8 Number of credit card holders in the United States: ....

③ What about you?

Could you (or do you) live without "magic plastic"? Discuss the advantages and disadvantages of credit cards with your group.

⑤ Internet

Of course, you can also shop on the Internet. Does anyone have any experience of this? How has it worked out? What good advice is there?

④ Mail order

Complete the form with your own information.

> **20TH CENTURY TOP 50!** – 2 exclusive CDs with the 50 absolute top songs of the last century. You'll never know how wonderful they still are until you hear them in this re-engineered digital version. Not sold in stores. Order by mail now! Just complete and send the form below.
>
> **20TH CENTURY TOP 50! * * * * CD EXPRESS * * * * ORDER FORM**
>
> Last name(s) .... First name(s) .... Mr ☐ Mrs ☐ Miss ☐ Ms ☐
>
> Address (street and number) ....
>
> .... City and country .... Zip code ....
>
> Telephone .... Fax .... E-mail ....
>
> Number of sets you want (each set consists of 2 CDs) ....
>
> Form of payment: Check ☐   Money order ☐   Credit card (details below) ☐
>
> Credit card: American Express ☐   MasterCard ☐   Visa ☐   Diners Club ☐
>
> Expiry date: Month ☐☐ Day ☐☐ Year ☐☐   Card number ☐☐☐☐ ☐☐☐☐ ☐☐☐☐ ☐☐☐☐
>
> Cardholder's name .... Signature ....
>
> We would really appreciate your answers to these questions:
>
> Are the CDs for yourself or for someone else? ....
>
> Why are you buying these CDs? ....

Check your completed form with a partner. Have you interpreted everything the same way? Would you really like these CDs for yourself or someone else? Why or why not?

1 Learning check

1 Progress check

a Complete the paragraph using the verbs in parentheses.

Canada (**1**) .... (*exist*) as a nation since 1867. Initially, it (**2**) .... (*consist*) of four provinces: Ontario, Quebec, New Brunswick and Nova Scotia. But at the time of independence, immigrants (**3**) .... (*move*) fast into the west, and soon new provinces (**4**) .... (*add*), beginning with Manitoba in 1870 and British Columbia in 1871. Canada now has 10 provinces and three territories. Nunavut, an autonomous Inuit or Eskimo territory, (**5**) .... (*establish*) in 1999.

b Select appropriate completions for the conversation.

Jill: Tell me about that article (**6**) .... about Nunavut.
      a) that read   **b)** who read   **c)** you read

Jack: Sure. Do you know what (**7**) ....? Only 25,000! That's really tiny for a territory
      a) large is the population   **b)** the population is   **c)** is the population
      (**8**) .... larger than Argentina.
      a) who's   **b)** which it's   **c)** that's

Jill: Larger than Argentina? Do you really know how big (**9**) ....? Or Argentina?
      a) does Nunavut have   **b)** is Nunavut   **c)** Nunavut is

Jack: That's what the article says. Anyway, if I (**10**) .... an Inuit, I'd feel happy about Nunavut.
      a) were   **b)** am   **c)** would be

Jill: Yes. But what's (**11**) .... to improve the Inuits' lives?
      a) been doing   **b)** being done   **c)** be done

Jack: I can't remember. If I find the article, (**12**) .... it to you.
      a) I'll give   **b)** I give   **c)** I'd give

c Write a compound word (e.g. *classroom* or *compact disc*) for each definition.

13 A .... is a place to buy stamps and mail letters.
14 .... is what you do to keep your home clean and tidy.
15 An .... is a place where anyone can go to use the Internet.

2 Proficiency check

a **Read sentences 1–5, below. Then listen to the interview, and select the best completion (a–c) for each sentence. You will hear the interview only once.**

1 Ms. Pérez is applying for:
   a) a promotion.
   b) a scholarship.
   c) a job.

2 Her subject is:
   a) physics.
   b) sociology.
   c) psychology.

3 She is interested in:
   a) research and practice.
   b) practice.
   c) research.

4 Her area of interest is:
   a) education.
   b) industry.
   c) occupational therapy.

5 She is going to explain:
   a) her needs.
   b) her special interests.
   c) her strong points.

b **Read the passage. Then read the questions and select the best answers.**

You should now be able to use English reasonably well in many real situations outside the classroom, for example:

- understanding announcements or simple presentations
- talking with foreigners in your own country or abroad
- reading for study, work or general interest; writing e-mails, letters or simple reports.

Many institutions of higher education and companies require candidates for a course, scholarship or job to prove their ability to use English for real communication. This usually means taking some kind of proficiency test. These tests check not only what you have just studied, but also all the English you have accumulated – your general proficiency in the language and your ability to communicate in real situations.

The Proficiency check section of Skyline will help you begin to prepare for widely accepted proficiency tests like TOEFL and Cambridge.

1 What is the main purpose of the whole text?
   a) To encourage you to use English outside the classroom.
   b) To explain the function of the "Proficiency check" section of this book.
   c) To discuss the use of English in study and work.

2 What is the main idea of the first paragraph?
   a) Your knowledge of English grammar is now almost complete.
   b) You now have to speak English outside the classroom a lot.
   c) Your English should now be good enough for many practical purposes.

3 What is the main idea of the second paragraph?
   a) To continue your studies or to work, you may need to pass a proficiency test.
   b) Colleges, companies, etc. have to use English proficiency tests now.
   c) Proficiency tests do not test what you have just learned.

4 *Abroad* in line 4 of paragraph 1 means:
   a) in another city.
   b) outside the classroom.
   c) not in your country.

5 *This* in line 2 of paragraph 2 refers to:
   a) proving ability to really use English.
   b) a course, scholarship or job.
   c) real communication in English.

Unit 3 Keeping up with technology

1 Developing the automobile

1 Speaking

a In pairs or groups, discuss the following questions.

1 Do you have a car? If so, what do you use it for? If not, what would you like to use one for?

2 What kind of problems do cars cause in big cities?

b Which of the cars on the right would you like to own? Why?

2 Reading and speaking

a In pairs, answer these questions, guessing if necessary.

1 Have there been gasoline-powered motor vehicles for more than 100 years or less?

2 Were cars in 2000 technically very different from cars in 1970 or virtually the same?

3 Which state in the United States took the lead in moving toward non-polluting vehicles – California, Illinois or New York?

4 Will non-polluting vehicles ever be as satisfactory in general performance as gasoline-powered cars?

b Read the following magazine article and check your answers to exercise 2a.

WHY CHANGE FROM GASOLINE ENGINES?

Automobiles have come a long way since Carl Benz built the first practical gasoline-powered motor vehicle in 1885. Over the first seven decades of the 20th century they became increasingly fast, comfortable, safe and reliable. Most of them also became much less expensive, so more and more people could afford one, new or secondhand.

By 1970 little technical improvement of automobiles seemed possible. However, by the end of the century virtually any new car could cruise safely at 20 miles an hour faster, using less gasoline and producing 80% less pollution than a new 1970 car. This was the result of using new technology such as fuel injection, multi-valve cylinders, and above all, microprocessors (or minicomputers).

But even today's cars produce about 50,000 kilograms of pollutants annually, mostly carbon monoxide and ozone, and every day there are more motor vehicles. Most people realize this is leading towards an ecological and human health disaster and some governments have been pushing automobile manufacturers to produce clean alternatives to the gas engine. In California, 10% of all new cars from 2003 have to be ZEVs (Zero Emission Vehicles) and that quota will increase progressively.

The first electric ZEVs were slow, limited in range, and very expensive compared with conventional cars, but that will soon change. The automobile industry is exploring different technologies, and several breakthroughs are close. More new cars are sold in California annually than in most countries, so this will have an impact everywhere. A change in the global market will then lead to mass production and reduced cost. One day soon, your city will be a quiet, pollution-free place, and ZEVs will be better than gas-engine vehicles in every way.

c Note at least three facts you have learned from reading this article. Compare your notes with a partner.

3 Reading, listening and speaking

a Read the following statements. Mark the statements T (true) or F (false).

1 ZEVs (Zero Emission Vehicles) will never be able to go as fast as gasoline-engine vehicles. T◯ F◯
2 Some ZEVs will be able to go farther than gasoline-engine vehicles without refueling. T◯ F◯
3 The best option for the development of ZEVs is new types of electric battery. T◯ F◯
4 ZEVs will soon be more economical than gasoline-engine vehicles. T◯ F◯
5 ZEVs are expensive at present because they are not mass produced. T◯ F◯

b Listen to an interview about ZEVs and check your answers.

c Listen again and complete the chart.

	Gasoline vehicles	ZEVs
source of energy		
level of pollution		
amount of noise		
cost		
speed		

d What have authorities in your country done to reduce pollution from vehicles? Imagine you are responsible for reducing vehicle pollution in your city. Make a list of five ideas to attack the problem of vehicle pollution.

4 Pronunciation: contrastive stress

a Look at the two sentences below from the interview. The two words in (1) that have the strongest stress or emphasis are underlined. Why are those two words stressed? Underline the two words in (2) with the strongest stress.

1 Don't forget the noise pollution as well as the air pollution.
2 Just imagine the quiet cities of the future compared with the noisy ones today.

b Listen to these sentences, and check the stressed words in 4a. Practice saying the two sentences.

c In pairs, discuss your ideas about the following things.

1 Big cars and small ones
2 Public transportation and private cars

2 Communications systems

1 Speaking

a Talk to the people in your class. Find people who do these things.

- spend more than one hour on the telephone every day
- listen to the radio a lot
- spend more than two hours watching television every day
- spend more than two hours using a computer every day
- have a cellular telephone
- have an e-mail address

Check (✔) each of the statements every time a student says *yes*.

b In groups of three or four, discuss what you found out from the questionnaire. Summarize your conclusions by writing *Everybody*, *Most people*, *Very few people* or *Nobody* beside each statement.

Most people spend more than one hour on the telephone every day.

2 Reading and speaking

a Read the three topic sentences below, and then read the article. Match each topic sentence with the appropriate paragraph.

1 But in our natural excitement over this constant development of electronic media, we should not forget that most people in the world don't have a telephone, and many don't even have electricity or clean water. ○

2 Almost all households in the U.S. today have at least three pieces of electronic communications equipment: a radio, a television and a telephone. ○

3 Major electronics companies are already working on the next generation in communications technology – combining all these modes of communication. ○

> **Learning tip:**
> using topic sentences
>
> - When you read a text, the topic sentence gives the reader the main idea in each paragraph.
> - The topic sentence is almost always the first sentence in a paragraph. The other sentences give more details or examples.

ACCESS TO TECHNOLOGY

a)
At least one third of American households also have a computer connected to the Internet. In addition, more than one in every five adults has a cell phone, and more and more people have some kind of portable computer which connects to the Internet.

b)
There will soon be fast, functional and widely affordable mobile "media phones" that will give you telephone, television and Internet all in one. And at home your telephone (or videophone) will also have a television and computer with Internet in a single apparatus. And it won't end there.

c)

Using a cell phone or handheld computer doesn't make you an Aristotle, Galileo or Einstein, whose achievements were made without the help of computers and the Internet. Living "off-line" is still the essential human condition.

b Decide which of the three paragraphs contains the writer's main point. What is that point? Compare and discuss your ideas with two or three partners.

c Work in groups of three or four. What are the main differences in technology between your generation and your parents' when they were your age? What are the main advantages and disadvantages of these changes?

I don't have a cell phone, but I know how to use one. My parents have no idea!

3 Grammar builder: gerunds

Gerunds are nouns that take the **–ing** form.

Smoking *is bad for you.*

a Underline the gerund phrases below. The first one has been done for you.

1 <u>Storing energy in batteries</u> is a problem at present.

2 Traveling by ZEV will be cheap.

3 Using a portable computer doesn't make you an Aristotle, Galileo or Einstein.

4 Our best hope for the future is creative thinking.

b Substitute the underlined words below with gerund phrases. The first one has been done for you.

1 <u>Sea travel</u> is uncommon nowadays.   Traveling by sea

2 <u>Night work</u> is usually very inconvenient.   ....

3 <u>City life</u> can be dangerous.   ....

4 A lot of investment goes into <u>technology development</u>.   ....

c Work in pairs. Student A look at column A and student B look at column B. Read each sentence to your partner and say if you agree or disagree with the statement and why.

Using computers doesn't improve your life.   *No, I don't agree. Using computers is really useful.*
       For example, you can bank on the Net 24 hours a day.

Column A

Surfing the Internet is a waste of time.
Playing video games makes kids hyperactive.

Column B

Using cell phones is usually unnecessary.
Watching TV is an escape from reality.

3 Using technology

1 Listening and speaking

a Work in pairs. Identify the appliances in the pictures using the words in the list below. Put them in order of most useful to least useful. Compare your list with another pair and give the reasons for your choices.

- a microwave oven ○
- a dishwasher ○
- an airconditioning / heating unit ○
- an electric toothbrush ○
- a videocassette recorder ○

b An 80-year-old man and his 18-year-old granddaughter are talking in the kitchen. Listen to their conversation and answer these questions.

1 How does the grandfather feel?
2 What is his attitude toward technology?
3 How does the granddaughter feel?
4 What is her attitude toward technology?

c Listen to the conversation again and answer these questions.

1 What is the grandfather trying to do?
2 Why is he having a problem?
3 What sequence of buttons should he be pressing?
4 The final time, what does he forget to include?

d The grandfather says "The trouble with technology is that it makes life easier but more impersonal. People don't talk to each other anymore." What do you think? Discuss your ideas in groups.

2 Pronunciation: intonation – question tags

a Listen to the intonation in the following two sentences. In the first one the speaker is sure and the intonation on the question tag falls. In the second, the speaker is unsure and the intonation on the question tag rises.

1 *This soup's hot, isn't it?* (Sure)

2 *You didn't resign, did you?* (Unsure)

b Now listen to these four sentences from the conversation in exercise 1. Decide if the speaker is sure (S) or unsure (U).

1 <u>You press</u> CLEAR first, <u>don't you</u>?　○
2 <u>I could</u> do it faster on the stove, <u>couldn't I</u>?　○

3 <u>It hasn't</u> started, <u>has it</u>?　○
4 <u>It just won't</u> work for me, <u>will it</u>?　○

3 Grammar builder: question tags

a Notice the grammar form in the examples in exercise 2b. Write question tags for the following sentences. Then listen and check your answers.

1　New technology makes life easier, ... ?
2　Modern technology really began in the 19th century, ... ?
3　Technology will develop faster and faster, ... ?
4　You don't use a computer much, ... ?
5　Most people can't afford the latest technology, ... ?
6　You're an electronic engineer, ... ?
7　You didn't press CLEAR, ... ?

b How do you express question tags in your language? Think about intonation and grammar.

4 Speaking, reading and writing

a How difficult or easy is it to use each of the following items?

- a camera
- a cell phone
- a computer
- a photocopier

Talk about any experiences you have had.

b Read the text on the right quickly, and write the function of each of the features of this product in the picture.

c Which words from the text show the order of the instructions? Underline each one.

d Choose one thing from the following list that you would like to be able to do. Find someone who can explain what to do, and write down his or her instructions.

1　Store a telephone number on a cell phone.
2　Set the alarm on a digital watch.
3　Program a VCR to record your favorite program.
4　Heat up some soup in a microwave oven.

It's easy. First you ...

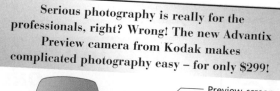
Serious photography is really for the professionals, right? Wrong! The new Advantix Preview camera from Kodak makes complicated photography easy – for only $299!

Preview screen
to see pictures you have taken

Preview button
....
....

Select button
....
....

Mode button
....
....

The main advantage of this model is the LCD (Liquid Crystal Display) screen that lets you preview your pictures by pressing the preview button. First you take your picture, then you can choose to make it wider or narrower. When you have the photograph you really want, you "select" it to print it. Finally, if you want reprints, you can copy as many as you want by using the mode button.

LANGUAGE for life:
learning on *the Web*

① Online courses

Online courses are becoming increasingly popular. How much do you know about them? For example, how are they similar to and different from traditional courses? And what about the jargon? What do these things refer to?

CHAT ROOMS	DISCUSSION PAGE
COURSE CONTENTS	QUIZZES AND TESTS
PRIVATE MAIL	COURSE CALENDAR

Match each of the areas above to the spaces in the text below. Check your answers with another student.

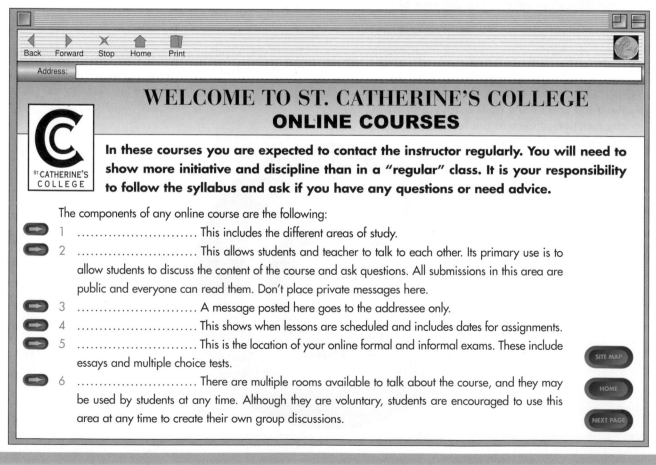

Back   Forward   Stop   Home   Print

Address:

WELCOME TO ST. CATHERINE'S COLLEGE
ONLINE COURSES

In these courses you are expected to contact the instructor regularly. You will need to show more initiative and discipline than in a "regular" class. It is your responsibility to follow the syllabus and ask if you have any questions or need advice.

The components of any online course are the following:

1 .... This includes the different areas of study.

2 .... This allows students and teacher to talk to each other. Its primary use is to allow students to discuss the content of the course and ask questions. All submissions in this area are public and everyone can read them. Don't place private messages here.

3 .... A message posted here goes to the addressee only.

4 .... This shows when lessons are scheduled and includes dates for assignments.

5 .... This is the location of your online formal and informal exams. These include essays and multiple choice tests.

6 .... There are multiple rooms available to talk about the course, and they may be used by students at any time. Although they are voluntary, students are encouraged to use this area at any time to create their own group discussions.

SITE MAP

HOME

NEXT PAGE

Read about online courses again. Mark the following statements T (true) or F (false).

1 In an online course you need to be responsible for organizing your own learning.   T◯ F◯
2 You can talk about personal problems on the discussion page.   T◯ F◯
3 Private mail is an open forum for all the people on your course.   T◯ F◯
4 To check when your assignments have to be ready, look at the course calendar.   T◯ F◯
5 All the writing tests are formal.   T◯ F◯
6 The chat room is compulsory.   T◯ F◯

And how about you? Would you be interested in taking an online course? Why or why not?

② Distance learning

Listen to the first part of an interview about distance learning and answer the following questions.

1 What is the topic of the radio program?
2 What does Alan Martin do at Bedford College?
3 What kind of courses is he going to talk about?

Listen to the second part of the interview and complete the notes below.

ONLINE COURSES:
Type of courses: vocational courses, ..., college ...., cooking and wine.
Cost: .... than classroom courses.
Advantages over traditional classroom courses: you can study when you have .... and .... this with other activities. You can do the course at your own ...., fast or ....
Instruction: by ...., course Web page and online classrooms.
Testing: you can take exams .... or off-site.
Reasons for failing: 1) you need a high level of self .... 2) many people like to have personal ....

Read this e-mail from Kenny to his friend, and write a reply using the notes above.

Back Forward Stop Home Print Mail
Address:

Hi _____
I think you wrote me a month ago, didn't you? So sorry this is late. Anyway, how are things going?
I've been very busy. I finished school in July and I have a part-time job with a design studio. It's really interesting and I'm looking for a course in computer design. I don't have much money to pay for a course, or time either. You did a distance learning course, right? Can you do me a favor and give me some information and advice about online courses? Mail me with your news and the info about the course!
All the best,
Kenny

Unit 4 House and home

1 Home away from home

1 Speaking and listening

a Look at the three photographs and identify the different types of accommodations. What are the good and bad points about each place?

b Listen to a student talking with her brother on the telephone. Check (✔) the points she mentions from the list.

courses ◯	music ◯	apartment ◯
friends ◯	food ◯	TV ◯
parties ◯	sports ◯	e-mail ◯

c Listen to the conversation again and answer the questions.

1 Why isn't Lilly living at home?
2 Where's she living?
3 What extra classes is she taking?
4 How is she feeling?

2 Pronunciation: intonation in questions

a Listen to these questions from the conversation in exercise 1 and notice the intonation. Why do you think the intonation changes?

1 *How are you doing?*

2 *Can you do that?*

3 *But what will Mom and Dad say?*

4 *Are they in?*

b **Work in pairs. Practice asking the following questions with the right intonation. Then listen and check your answers.**

1 What time are we going shopping?
2 Is this table new?
3 Where did you put the brochure?
4 Do you want to change the wallpaper?

3 Speaking and reading

a **In pairs or groups, discuss this question.**
Where do college students normally live in your country?

b **The University of California at Los Angeles has four apartment buildings for students. Read the students' questions below. Then read the UCLA website and answer the questions.**

1 Are the university apartment buildings on, near or some distance from the campus?
2 Do I have to buy any furniture?
3 Do I have to share an apartment with another person?
4 What kind of cooking and cleaning facilities are there?
5 If I apply for an apartment, will I get one?
6 What is the shortest period I can rent an apartment?
7 How can I get more information about the apartments?

| ◀ Back | ▶ Forward | ✕ Stop | ⌂ Home | Print |

Address:

UCLA owns and operates four apartment buildings located off campus, each only minutes walking distance from the University. The apartments are fully furnished units, with studio, one-, two- and three-bedroom options. All have full kitchens, and some are air-conditioned. Each building has coin-operated washers and dryers. Students are assigned to these apartments on a space-available basis. Student contracts are for the entire academic year.

For an application or for more information, write, phone, fax or e-mail: UCLA Housing Assignment Office, 270 DeNeve Drive, Los Angeles, CA 90095-1387. Tel: (310) 825-4271, Fax: (310) 825-8839 E-mail: uan@ha.ucla.edu

c **Work in groups of three. Discuss the advantages of these different types of accommodations for college students: apartments, rooms on campus, living at home.**

4 Word builder: interiors

a **Form two groups, A and B. Group A look at picture 1 and group B look at picture 2. Write the names of the items shown in each room.**

b **Which items are in the wrong room and where should they go?**
The garden fork shouldn't be there. It should be in the ......

c **Work in pairs with a student from the other group and exchange information about your rooms.**

2 Decoration

1 Speaking and listening

a Look at this picture of a room. What would you change to make it look nicer? Discuss your ideas with another student.

b Listen to the conversation between two people and answer these questions.

   1 Who decorated the apartment?

   2 What does James think of the decoration?

   3 One thing doesn't need changing. What is it?

   4 What's the problem about redecorating the apartment?

c Listen to the conversation again and complete the details for redecorating the apartment.

Area	Change
1 walls	....
2	Throw it out and get something to match the walls.
3 lighting	....
4	You couldn't give it away.
5 floor	....
6	Take them down and look for some posters.

2 Speaking and reading

a What are the main things that affect the decoration of a room? Discuss your ideas in groups of three. Then read the following article on interior decoration quickly to check your answers.

*T*hree key elements in home interior decoration are the use of space, the use of light and color and the use of decorative objects of personal significance to the people who live in the home. However, personal taste and the specific use of a room or area of the house can influence decoration.

A teenager's (1) .... is usually a very private space into which few people are invited. It may be decorated in a way that horrifies the parents but thrills the youngster; the shelves covered with all sorts of objects and sentimental or shocking posters on the walls. The use of the room and the taste displayed in it are highly personal.

A (2) .... is essentially a functional space used for preparing and eating food. Many families eat there on a daily basis and use the dining room for more formal occasions. These days, they are usually colorful and designed to make life easier.

The (3) .... is a more public place, and may be carefully designed to make guests feel comfortable, and perhaps to impress them a little. The decoration, therefore, considers other people's tastes, and goes for many common denominators

rather than purely personal or idiosyncratic options. There are likely to be fairly conventional pictures, ceramic objects and ornamental lampshades.

b Read the article again and fill in the spaces with the name of the correct room.

c Complete the diagram of the article's structure and content. Compare your completed diagrams in pairs or groups.

Three key elements in home interior decoration are:

1 ....

2 <u>Light and color</u>

3 ....

Main characteristic of each room or area described in the article:

Example 1: ....

Typical features:
<u>Private - highly personal</u>

Example 2: ....

Typical features:
....

Example 3: ....

Typical features:
....

d In pairs, describe and discuss a room you really like in your own house or a relative or friend's house. What makes it so special?

3 **Grammar builder:** multi-word verbs

Some multi-word verbs have an object:

Throw out <u>*the furniture*</u>.

Others don't:

He ***moved out***.

a Look at the multi-word verbs in italics in the sentences below. Underline the verbs with an object, and put a circle round those without an object. The first three have been done for you.

1 I'll <u>*look after*</u> the dog while you're away.

2 Prices of houses and apartments do not often (*go down.*)

3 I wish the neighbors would <u>*turn*</u> their TV <u>*down*</u>.

4 There are tools all over the floor. *Put* them *away* before you go to bed.

5 They *gave away* their old car.

6 We should *take down* that old bathroom mirror.

7 I've *turned* the water *off*.

8 The candle *went out*.

b Classify the multi-word verbs used above according to type.

Type 1:	Type 2:	Type 3:
two parts, with a final object	two parts, without an object	two parts, with a middle or final object
look after (the dog)	go down	turn (the TV) down / down (the TV)
....	....	....

35

3 Street scenes

1 Listening and speaking

a In pairs or groups, compare the two scenes on the right. What are the similarities and the differences between them?

b Listen to two people talking about where they live. Look at the scenes on the right, and list the things in the scenes they mention. Compare your answers in pairs.

c Listen to the conversation again, and check (✔) points about the neighborhood you hear mentioned.

1 The elevator sometimes breaks down.
2 Children played on the street when there were houses.
3 There's a lot of vandalism in the apartments.
4 You don't meet many people in the apartment building.
5 There were lots of parties on the old street.
6 The old houses had small yards.
7 The play area at the apartments isn't very clean.
8 The apartments only have one bedroom each.

d Problem solving. Work in groups of three. Look again at the second street scene. How would you improve things? Imagine you have a budget of $120,000. Decide how you would use it to make conditions better for the residents.

2 Grammar builder: *used to* and *would*

a Look at examples 1–3 from the conversation in exercise 1. Match the questions with the examples.

1 I **used to see** my neighbors almost every day.
2 The kids **would play** on the street except in winter.
3 You know I **used to have** a dog.

a Which examples talk about habits in the past? ………
b Which example talks about a state in the past? ………
c In which example (1 or 3) is it **not** possible to use *would*? ………

b Decide, in each of the sentences below, if it is possible to use both *would* and *used to* or only *used to*.

1 At my grandma's house we *used to / would* eat a lot of cake.
2 We *used to / would* live in an apartment.
3 When we were children we *used to / would* go swimming every weekend.
4 Tim *used to / would* smoke a lot at college.
5 The Simpsons *used to / would* play on a football team at college.

c Write two true and two false statements about your past, using *used to* and *would*. Work with a partner and guess which are true and which are false.

A: I used to work in a movie studio. *B: Really! I don't believe you.*

d Work in groups. Talk about how things have changed where you live.

3 Speaking, reading and writing

a Work in groups of three. Look at the photograph below and describe it.

b Read the article and match the photograph to a paragraph. Guess the names of the other three places.

STREET SCENES

Every country has its street life which is influenced by factors such as climate, culture, the economy and urban development.

1 In some countries street cafés are a common feature where, especially in summer, people sit outside to drink coffee, chat, eat and watch the world go by. In some cases you pay more for food and drinks if you sit down than if you stand up at the bar.

2 In this famous city the streets are canals and people move from place to place by boat or gondola. This situation is due to the city being built on a lagoon with 400 bridges linking 118 separate islands. Boats of all shapes and sizes transport people and goods, and even act as ambulances.

3 Because of religious beliefs, cows are a common feature of street life in this country. As they are sacred they can walk where they want and even eat the vegetables from market stalls without the owners doing anything. Streets are normally crowded with buses, rickshaws and bicycles.

4 This city has such tall buildings that the sun is blocked out from the streets. The Empire State

Building has 102 stories and can house 14,000 workers. Although there are lots of stores and places where you can buy newspapers and flowers, most activity is inside or underground because of the extremely cold winters.

c Read the following list of items, and identify in which paragraphs in the article above they appear. Some appear in more than one paragraph.

1 forms of transport: 2 & 3

2 bridges:

3 sacred animals:

4 outdoor cafés:

5 big buildings with thousands of workers:

6 boats:

7 markets:

8 underground areas to avoid the cold weather:

d In pairs, write a short description of a typical street in your town or country. Look at exercise 3c for ideas.

places to *stay*

① Vacation choices

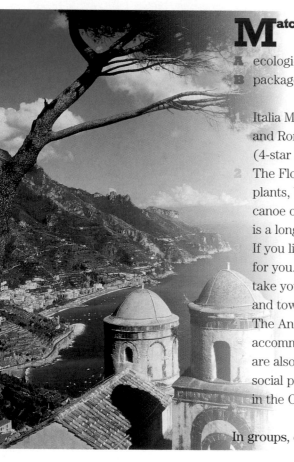

Match the different types of vacation, a–d, with descriptions 1–4.

A ecological vacation   **C** cruise

B package tour   **D** adventure vacation

1 Italia Mia. Eight days all inclusive. Visit Milan, Venice, Florence and Rome. Price includes airfare, food and accommodations (4-star hotels). ○

2 The Florida Everglades offer a vast natural space full of plants, birds and wildlife. Ideal for nature lovers, you can canoe or travel by boat to remote areas where civilization is a long way away. ○

If you like playing around with boats, Sail Away is the vacation for you. Our experienced instructors will teach you to sail and take you along the California coast to visit wonderful beaches and towns. Water skiing and diving are available. ○

The Andrea Doria is waiting for you. Passengers have 5-star accommodations and nine restaurants to choose from. There are also swimming pools, gymnasiums, a movie theater, a full social program plus visits to some of the most beautiful places in the Caribbean. ○

In groups, decide on one vacation that you will all take.

② Timesharing

Ever heard of timesharing vacations? Yes? No? What do you know about them? Discuss the question then read the text quickly and check your answer.

WHY TIMESHARING WORKS

Until timesharing came about, most Americans had only two main alternatives for taking vacations: rent a hotel room with constantly increasing rates, reservation hassles and none of the comforts of home, or own a resort home or condominium which costs a lot of money and which you would probably only use a couple of weeks a year.

But that has changed with a new business – timeshares. With timeshares you sell 51 weeks of the year to 51 owners. This means that timeshare owners can afford a nicer place as the cost is divided between lots of people. Annual expenses are much less because they are shared and the apartment is occupied all year, which also reduces costs.

With timeshares, clients buy a week for life in a resort. They and their families can use this during the lifetime of the owner. The timesharer pays maintenance costs and utilities (water, electricity and telephone). With some companies, the timeshare owner can exchange his or her week for a week in another resort, or even rent the week if he or she doesn't want to use it.

Read the text again and answer T (true) or F (false) to the following statements.

1 The article suggests the two normal vacation alternatives are unsatisfactory. T ◯ F ◯

2 People who own vacation homes use them intensively. T ◯ F ◯

3 Timeshare companies rent every week of the year to different people. T ◯ F ◯

4 Timeshare owners don't pay for anything except the cost of the week they buy. T ◯ F ◯

5 You buy a timeshare for a number of years. T ◯ F ◯

6 You can always change your week for a different week if you want. T ◯ F ◯

Learning tip: working out meaning of new words

● When you read a text quickly for general understanding (as in first part of exercise 2), don't worry about individual words you don't understand. When you read more carefully (as in True/False exercise), you will need to guess some words because they are important for understanding the text.

● In these cases, try to work out:
a) the type of word it is – adjective, noun, adverb, verb;
b) how it fits in with the rest of the sentence, especially the theme or topic;
c) if it is similar to a word in your own language;
d) what kind of word you could put in its place.

---

③ Clinching a sale

Listen to the conversation between Angie Brown of Worldwide Vacations and Mr. Turner, a client, and answer the following questions.

1 Where did the client see the information about the timeshare?

2 Who have the Turners talked to?

Listen to the conversation again and complete the form.

WORLDWIDE VACATIONS

Timesharing information card

Rep.: Angie Brown   Date: 8/17/01

Client: Carl

Last name: ....

First name(s): ....

Address: ....

Street: .... Number: ....

City: .... State: Illinois ....

Zip code: ....

Telephone: (645) ....

E-mail: ....

Resort: .... Town: ....

Country: .... Week: ....

Total cost: US$ ....

Maintenance cost: US$ ....

Form of payment: Check ☐

Credit card: Visa ☐   Diners ☐

American Express ☐

Card details: ....

Card number: 3789 2378 2874 3289

Expiration date: ....

Work in groups of three and answer the following questions.

1 Where would you like to have a timeshare?

2 Are timeshares common in your country?

2 Learning check

1 Progress check

a Rewrite each of the sentences replacing the underlined verbs with the correct form of one of the multi-word verbs in the box.

1 Prices for computers have <u>fallen</u>.

   ....

2 Production of microchips is <u>increasing</u>.

   ....

3 She's <u>managing</u> very well in her new job.

   ....

4 I need to <u>learn</u> more about word processing.

   ....

5 They had to <u>lower</u> the volume of the microphone.

   ....

> get along
> go down
> turn down
> find out
> go up

b Complete the instructions using a suitable word from the lists below.

To use a CD player, first you have to (**6**) .... it on. (**7**) .... you select "CD" from the controls and (**8**) .... "OPEN." After (**9**) .... a CD, you put it in the tray and press "CLOSE." (**10**) .... , you push "PLAY" and listen to the music.

6	**a)** connect	**b)** find	**c)** turn	**d)** move
7	**a)** After	**b)** Then	**c)** Finally	**d)** Before
8	**a)** pull	**b)** lift	**c)** take	**d)** press
9	**a)** cleaning	**b)** choosing	**c)** deciding	**d)** looking
10	**a)** Last	**b)** Finally	**c)** Second	**d)** After

c Read the text below and look carefully at each line. Some of the lines are correct and some have a word that should not be there. Check (✔) the correct lines or write the words that should not be there.

Sony has introduced the world's first only robot pet.   ....only.......
AIBO (Artificial Intelligence Robot) costs $2000   ......✔..........
11 and is the first of a whole complete menagerie of   ....
12 artificial pets. The robot has only modest abilities.   ....
13 For example, it can bark itself for attention   ....
14 and sit up or lie down. It can't no understand   ....
15 orders or bring you the newspaper in the morning.   ....

2 Proficiency check

a Look at the booking form about the Sotwell Inn Hotel. Then listen to the telephone conversation and complete the information.

SOTWELL INN HOTEL
BOOKING FORM

Name of customer: First: ..ALEX......................   Last: ....

Number of nights: ....   Dates: ....

Type of room: single ☐   double ☐   suite ☐

Cost per night: U.S.$ ....   Price includes: ....

Form of payment: cash ☐   credit card ☐ (American Express   Visa   MasterCard)

---

b Read the passage. Then read the questions and statements and select the best answers.

Americans Spend a Scary Amount on Halloween

Halloween is a huge celebration in America and this year is expected to be bigger than most. The statistics themselves are scary. The average American adult is expected to spend $43 on celebrating October 31, making Halloween the second biggest holiday after Christmas in terms of dollars spent.

Most of the money (an estimated $1.9 billion) will be spent on candy. In a survey carried out by American Demographics last year, seven out of ten Americans said they would be handing out treats to ward off tricks. The demand is so great that 20% of all confectionery bought in the United States is purchased in the two months before October 31.

An estimated $1.5 billion is also expected to be spent on costumes. If you include candy, costumes, decorations and cards, the Halloween Association estimates $6 billion will be spent this year, up from $5 billion last year. Hallmark sells about 23 million Halloween cards every year.

What is the fascination with Halloween? Partly it is because of economic prosperity and partly because of a general fascination with the different elements of Halloween: witches, ghosts, monsters and pagan rituals. And it's not just limited to children. Between 40% and 60% of all adults between the ages of 18 and 44 said they intended to dress up for Halloween; 8% said they intended to dress their pets as well!

1 What is the main theme of the text?
 a) Halloween customs in the United States.
 b) The popularity of Halloween.
 c) The amount of money spent on Halloween in the United States.
 d) The activities of the Halloween Association.

2 The article says that Halloween:
 a) is more popular than any other holiday.
 b) is a big holiday for children.
 c) is an official government holiday.
 d) is a holiday where people spend less than at Christmas.

3 During the Halloween period:
 a) most money is spent on cards and costumes.
 b) the U.S. confectionery industry sells a fifth of its annual sales.
 c) people spend too much.
 d) everyone sends Halloween cards.

4 For this year's Halloween, people:
 a) will spend 20% more than last year.
 b) will spend $1.5 billion on costumes.
 c) will buy all their cards from Hallmark.
 d) will pay a lot more for decorations.

5 People are fascinated with Halloween because:
 a) they want to escape from economic problems.
 b) they like dressing their pets in costumes.
 c) adults are less mature these days.
 d) they like the different elements involved in Halloween.

2 Crime and punishment

1 Speaking and reading

a In groups, discuss what you know about Australia.

b Read the book extract about Australia, below, and write the correct dates in statements 1–4.

1 .... : America gains its independence from Britain.

2 .... : first British settlement in Australia, Port Jackson.

3 .... : arrival of the last convicts in Australia.

4 .... : full independence of Australia.

THE BEGINNINGS OF MODERN AUSTRALIA

The first humans to settle in Australia came from south-eastern Asia and are called Aborigines, which means "the first people who lived in any country." Now the word is used mainly for native Australians.

The next big influx came thousands of years later when the British began to colonize Australia. This colonization was based on convict labor (work done by people who had previously been in prison). There were two reasons why convicts were deported to Australia: one was that Britain wanted to colonize Australia before the French did. The other reason was that America, where convicts used to be sent, was no longer a colony of Britain. (America gained its independence in 1776.)

The first place convicts were sent to was Port Jackson, which was established in 1788 and later became Sydney. Deportation, also called "transportation," to Sydney, only stopped in 1837 when a Parliamentary Committee Report strongly condemned the practice. However, it wasn't until 30 years later that the practice had stopped completely in Australia.

Many of the convicts had committed what would now be considered minor crimes, such as stealing food for a hungry family. Australia, which was at first their prison, later became for them a land of opportunity. It became a fully independent nation in 1901, only 34 years after the last convicts had arrived to serve their sentences.

c **Read the text again. Discuss these questions.**

1 Why were convicts taken all the way to Australia at the end of the 18th century?
2 Why was transportation to Port Jackson stopped?
3 What kind of crimes had most of the convicts committed?

2 Grammar builder: past perfect

a **Look at the following two sentences. Which two tenses are used? Which tense is used for the action / event that happened first, and which for the one that happened later?**

1 Parts of Australia still <u>received</u> convicts 30 years after the Committee <u>had presented</u> its report.

2 Australia <u>became</u> a fully independent nation only 34 years after the last convicts <u>had arrived</u>.

b **Read the first sentence of each pair and complete the second sentence of each pair, making sure it has the same meaning. Use the past perfect.**

1 The French considered colonizing Australia, but then the British established settlements there.
The French .... Australia before the British .... there.

2 Britain lost its American colonies, and then it began to send convicts to Australia.
After Britain .... its American colonies, it .... to Australia.

3 Many of the convicts committed minor crimes and then they were convicted.
Many of the convicts .... before they ....

> **Language assistant**
> In these kinds of examples, the past simple is often used for both past actions or events, but the past perfect emphasizes which one happened first.

3 Pronunciation: past tense forms

a **Look at the following past tense forms. Write them out as rhyming pairs.**

went	sent	drank	met	flew	bought	read
said	grew	made	sank	caught	let	paid

Notice that the spelling for the same sound is sometimes the same and sometimes different:

/e/ went met said

Notice also that the same spelling may represent more than one sound:

said /e/ paid /eɪ/

b **Check that you know the infinitive and the past participle for each of these verbs, and also the pronunciation of each form. Use a dictionary or the verb table at the back of the book to help you.**

3 Crime knows no borders

1 Speaking and reading

a In pairs, discuss the following five statements and decide if you think they are T (true) or F (false).

1 INTERPOL is an international police force. T ○ F ○
2 It is more than 100 years old. T ○ F ○
3 It is based in the United States. T ○ F ○
4 More than 150 countries are members. T ○ F ○
5 It investigates international criminal cases. T ○ F ○

b Read the text below, and check your ideas about INTERPOL.

INTERPOL is an international organization which has coordinated cooperation between the police forces of different countries since 1923. There were 177 member countries in 1997. The headquarters or General Secretariat is located in Lyon, France. INTERPOL is not itself a police force, and it does not conduct investigations. Cases are investigated by the national police forces of the member countries under their own laws, but INTERPOL plays a very important role in supplying criminal information from one country's police force to another.

2 Grammar builder: review of past tenses

Complete the text with an appropriate verb or verb phrase from the box.
Use each one only once.

lived	has lived	has been living	was living	had lived	used to live

INTERPOL gets its man

Melvin Patterson (1) .... in luxurious rented apartments in different parts of the world but since November 15, 2000, he (2) .... in a prison near Toronto. He (3) .... in almost all the capitals of Europe and Latin America as well as New York, and now Toronto.

He appeared to be a respectable businessman, but he was really a swindler, who tricked people into investing in companies which did not exist. From March to October, 2000, he (4) .... in a penthouse in Toronto. What he did not know was that a policeman (5) .... in the building across the street. In his computer he had a collection of photographs and descriptions of Patterson from the INTERPOL database collected from all the countries he (6) .... and swindled in. It was the end of the road for one more international criminal.

3 Speaking, writing and reading

a Imagine you are going to interview Melvin Patterson. In pairs, prepare some questions to ask the international criminal. Use the ideas below to help you.

1 How long have you .... ?
2 Have you ever .... ?
3 Before you were arrested had you .... ?
4 What was the biggest .... ?
5 When you were a boy did you use to .... ?
6 When was the first time you .... ?
7 Do you have any regrets?

b In pairs, conduct the interview. One of you is the reporter and one of you is Melvin Patterson. The reporter needs to take notes to write a newspaper article after the interview.

c In pairs, write a brief newspaper article of no more than 120 words based on the interview with Melvin Patterson.

d Read another article, written by another two students. How many similarities and how many differences can you find between the two articles?

4 Speaking, reading and listening

a What are drug trafficking and money laundering? What is the connection between the two crimes?

b Read the options listed below and predict which ones are correct. Then listen to a radio-talk and check your answers.

1 Drugs are produced in:
a) a few specific countries.   b) every country in the world.   c) many varying countries.

2 Drug trafficking routes:
a) are all well established.   b) include old and new ones.   c) are changing all the time.

3 Drug consumption is highest in:
a) rich countries.   b) poor countries.   c) countries that don't produce drugs.

4 Most money laundering is done through banks in:
a) large, poor countries.   b) small, rich countries.   c) large, rich countries.

c In groups, discuss one of the following international crime problems.

1 Drug trafficking.
2 The use of foreign banks to launder money – that is, to apparently "legalize" illegal money.
3 The escape of criminals to a country from which they cannot be extradited.

d When you are ready, each group should make a brief presentation of their ideas to the class.

LANGUAGE for life:
understanding *nations*

① Belonging

② Vive la différence!

They say we all need to belong. We usually begin by "belonging" with our mother, our father and our brothers and sisters. Then we belong with relatives and friends. Next, institutions invite us to belong too, our schools first. And at some point we realize that we belong to a much larger community – the nation. We feel loyalty toward it, and sometimes, unfortunately, hostility toward other nations.

What most makes you feel you belong to your nation? Is it:

- *the language, or even the accent or dialect?*
- *other cultural things like music, dance, food, festivals, religion?*
- *the physical appearance of the people or the way they behave?*
- *simply the fact that you were raised in your country and have many memories of it?*

Ask your friends in class what makes them feel they belong to their national community. How strongly do they feel about their region within their country?

Look at this picture of a suburb in Brisbane, Australia. What similarities and differences can you see between this scene and a similar scene in your own country?

What things do you find most attractive and most unattractive about this Australian city scene and a similar scene in your country?

③ Rules and regulations down under

The 2000 Summer Olympics drew enormous numbers of visitors to Sydney, Australia, from all round the world. Although it was the "summer" Olympics, it was still winter, or perhaps early spring, in Australia, the equivalent of March in the Northern Hemisphere. Other things were different for most of the visitors too.

What do you know about Australia? Answer this quiz.

VISAS

1 Which is the only country whose passport holders do not require a visa to visit Australia?

LANGUAGE – English, of course, but ...

2 What does "G'day" mean in Australian English?

3 What are the second and third most widely spoken languages in Australia?

4 What language do "boomerang" and "didgeridoo" come from, and what do they mean?

DRIVING

5 Do vehicles drive on the right or the left?

6 Is it compulsory to wear a seatbelt or not?

SMOKING

7 In which of the following places is smoking prohibited: government buildings, public transportation, airports?

GEOGRAPHY

8 What is the capital of Australia?

9 Where do most Australians live?

10 What type of land covers most of Australia?

Check your answers with the key below.

Answers: 1 New Zealand. 2 Good day (i.e. Good morning / afternoon, or simply Hello). 3 Second biggest language is Italian. Third biggest language is Greek. 4 Both words come from the Aborigines. A "boomerang" is a hunting weapon and a "didgeridoo" is a musical instrument. 5 Left. 6 Compulsory. 7 All of them. 8 Canberra. 9 Most people live on the coast. 10 Much of Australia is flat, dry desert.

④ Advice for a visitor

Listen to an Australian giving advice to an American who is going to visit Australia. Complete sentences 1–4, below, and discuss them with a friend.

1 Before crossing a street in Australia always ....

2 Before you make your trip to Australia ....

3 Visit different places a long way apart, for example:
   a) ....
   b) ....
   c) ....

4 For April, take .... clothes.

Would you like to visit Australia? If yes, why? If no, why not?

Imagine a friend from Australia is going to visit your city or region next month. Make brief notes and then write three short paragraphs about the following.

1 The weather, clothes, etc.

2 Places to visit and things to see and do.

3 Any customs that you think might be different, for example how people say hello to each other.

2 Investigative journalism

1 Speaking and reading

a Do you know the answers to the following questions? If you don't, try to find someone in the group who does. Then read the article about Watergate, below, and check the answers.

1 What are the names of the two big political parties in the United States?
2 Who is the only U.S. president ever to resign – Richard Nixon, Ronald Reagan or Bill Clinton?
3 Why did this president resign?

THE **WATERGATE** STORY

Watergate is still the biggest political scandal in American history. It is also one of the biggest newspaper stories of all time – a classic example of investigative journalism.

The basic facts are well known, and have been told in two movies, *All the President's Men* starring Robert Redford and Dustin Hoffman, and *Nixon* starring Anthony Hopkins and James Woods.

In June 1972, five men were arrested during a break-in at the Democratic Party's headquarters in the Watergate Building. Two young reporters of the Washington Post newspaper heard about these arrests, apparently insignificant, and published an article two days later. Republican President, Richard Nixon, insisted that he knew nothing about the break-in. But the reporters followed the story closer and closer to the White House.

Their big break was when an anonymous informant telephoned one of them, Bob Woodward, and told him that Nixon had directly ordered the break-in to spy on the opposition Democratic Party, and had tried to cover it up. He also said that Nixon kept recordings of all his meetings. The Investigating Committee demanded the tapes. Nixon said he would never hand them over, but was finally obliged to do so. They revealed that he was indeed behind the Watergate break-in and the cover-up.

In 1974, Nixon resigned, and Bob Woodward, the reporter, was famous.

Bob Woodward, the reporter who trapped a dishonest President

b Read the article again and answer these questions.

1 Which two movies are about the Watergate scandal?
2 What was the first indication that political spying was taking place?
3 What position did the President take about it?
4 Who began to investigate the story?
5 What was the big opening in their investigation?
6 How was the President's involvement confirmed?
7 What happened in 1974 as a consequence of the scandal?

c Have any big scandals been revealed by the media in your country?

2 **Grammar builder:** past reported speech – statements

a Look at the reported statements below, and compare them with the original statements. How have the verbs changed in the two versions? Are there similar changes in your language?

1 Nixon said he would never hand over the tapes.
"I will never hand over the tapes."

2 He insisted that he knew nothing about the break-in.
"I know nothing about the break-in. Nothing!"

3 An informant told Woodward that Nixon had ordered the break-in.
"Nixon ordered the break-in, Mr. Woodward."

4 He also said Nixon had tried to cover it up.
"Nixon has tried to cover it up."

b Read the first part of the pairs of sentences below, and complete the second part using reported speech.

1a) "I have told no lies about this matter," he said.

 b) He said he ....

2a) "I will resign here in the Oval Office tomorrow," he announced.

 b) He announced that he .... in the Oval Office the .... day.

3a) "My family understands," he told reporters.

 b) He told reporters that ....

4a) "I can be proud of my achievements as President," he insisted.

 b) He insisted he ....

Language assistant

- It is common to omit *that*, especially in speech:
He said (that) he would never hand over the tapes.

- In speech, we often use the original tense, especially when the situation is still happening:
She said she studies English (instead of: She said she studied English.)

---

3 **Speaking, writing and reading**

a Think of something terrible you did when you were younger. Share stories with at least three people. Write a brief report about the worst story you heard in your investigation.

Samantha told me she ...   She said that ...

b Read one another's reports in groups, and discuss them.

3 Ethical issues

1 Speaking, listening and reading

a In pairs, look at the photograph. What do you think about the paparazzi?

b Listen to a TV discussion program about news photographers. Who is closest to your opinions, the woman or the man?

c From your memory of the discussion, mark the following opinions as **W** (the woman's) or **M** (the man's). Listen again and check.

1 Most celebrities want attention at first, and should not complain later. ○
2 Everyone has the right to privacy, especially at home. ○
3 Celebrities should accept that fame means loss of privacy. ○
4 Laws that try to protect privacy are hard to enforce. ○
5 Censorship can interfere with serious investigative journalism. ○
6 There have to be laws against the invasion of privacy. ○

2 Grammar builder: past reported speech – questions

a Read the conversation below. Then look at the reported questions that follow and compare them with the original questions underlined. How many changes can you see?

Woman: There should be a law against taking photographs through private windows.

Man: Well, have you ever taken a photograph through someone else's window?

Woman: Uh ... well, maybe ... but it was a friend's house ...

Man: Ah, but how can you prove your friend's consent? Your friend might protest later.

He asked her if she had ever taken a photograph through someone else's window.

He asked her how she could prove her friend's consent.

b Read the first sentence of each pair, and complete the second sentence of each pair using the correct form of the verb for reported questions.

1 "Where do you live?" she asked him.
  She asked him where ....

2 "Can you stop photographing me?" she asked him.
  She asked him if ....

3 "What have you done to protect your privacy?" he asked her.
  He asked her what ....

4 "Will you let me take some photographs?" he asked her.
  He asked her if ....

3 Word builder: useful expressions for discussions

Complete the discussion below with appropriate expressions from the box.

I think	I don't think	don't you think	I agree	I don't agree	in my opinion

Woman: What about the harassment of celebrities by paparazzi?

Man: Well, (1) .... many celebrities complain too much. They want attention at first, then, when they're famous, they want it to stop.

Woman: But (2) .... everyone has the right to some privacy?

Man: Yes, (3) .... up to a point. But (4) .... , people who want fame should accept the sacrifice.

Woman: (5) .... at all. Privacy in one's own home should be an absolute right. There should be a law against taking photographs through private windows.

Man: Well, (6) .... it's possible to enforce a law like that.

4 Speaking and reading

a In groups, discuss these questions.

1 Do you think there should be censorship of violent or other material in the media?

2 Why or why not?

3 What do you think the kids are looking at in the picture below?

b Read the article below about censorship on the Internet. In general, whose side are you on – the smart kids or the concerned parents?

A VIRTUAL BATTLEGROUND

Most parents would like their children to succeed in life, and recognize that the Internet is one of the keys to success in the 21st century. So parents that are able to get a computer and Internet connection at home usually do. But most parents also realize that the Internet is a world of unrestricted information, communication and entertainment – including extreme violence, pornography and racist propaganda. They want their child to benefit from the information and fun, but they do not want them to wander into virtual "red-light" or crime zones any more than they would like them to wander into real red-light or crime zones in a city.

To help concerned parents control their children's access to the wide world of the Internet, software companies are offering many filter or "blocking programs" – family filters, "under-10 blocks," and so on. However, other groups, some supporting "freedom of speech," are working against such blocks and filters. One of these, *Peacefire*, offers children ways around their parents' filter or blocking programs. Their motto is: "It's not a crime to be smarter than your parents." They comment as follows: "An Associated Press story reports that 'only one in 20 children can evade computer filtering technology.' Good, let's keep the adults thinking that."

c In pairs, list advantages and disadvantages of free access to the Internet from the point of view of parents with children under the age of 15.

Advantages	Disadvantages

d Compare your list with another pair's, and discuss them. Then discuss this question.
Do you think it should be illegal to assist minors (under-18-year-olds) to get past Internet filters or blocks imposed by their parents?

LANGUAGE for life:
doing *research*

① When you desperately need to know

When was Abraham Lincoln President of the United States? Is the population of Nigeria greater or smaller than the population of Mexico? How many automobiles does Brazil export to the European Union? In study and work, we often need to know the answers to questions like these. How would you find the answers to the three questions above? Compare your research strategies with those of other people.

For the next time you meet, find the answers to the three questions, and compare them with other people's answers. Who found the answers quickly and easily?

② Researching Nigeria

What do you already know about Nigeria? What can you guess? What can you find out quickly?

Official name: The .... of Nigeria
Location: West ....
Area (km²): ....
Climate: .... in the south, and .... in the north.
Capital: ....
Population: ....
Languages: official – .... ; unofficial – Hausa, Fulani, Yoruba and Arabic
Main exports: ....

🎧 Like most nations, especially young ones, Nigeria has its problems, but most Nigerians are proud of their nation and optimistic about the future.

Listen to a Nigerian college lecturer giving a short talk about her country. See if you can complete the information on page 56.

The Internet

The Internet is the most powerful research machine in human history – and you ain't seen nothing yet, earthling! To use it, all you need is a few basic notions and then just explore!

How are you on the basic notions? See if you can match the notes to the search page – write the appropriate section number (in red) beside each note.

Have you done any research on the Internet? What was your experience? Compare your experience with that of your friends.

[3] Learning check

1 Progress check

a Complete the sentences with the correct past tense of the verbs in parentheses.

1 Elena .... (*live*) in Houston when she was a kid.

2 The train .... already .... (*leave*) when we arrived at the station.

3 We .... (*drive*) to the airport when Philip called to say he would be late.

4 Monica and Peter .... (*travel*) to Japan three times this year!

5 Sandra .... (*go*) to the same college as me.

6 I .... (*work*) on this report all morning and I still haven't finished.

7 .... you .... (*see*) the new Bruce Willis movie?

8 What .... Amanda .... (*do*) last night?

9 She .... (*not pass*) .... her driving test the first time.

b Read the first sentence of each pair. Complete the second sentence of each pair so it has the same meaning.

10 "I haven't seen Mandy for ages," he said.

He said ....

11 "We can't come to the party on Saturday," they told me.

They told me ....

12 "You have to call the office immediately," he insisted.

He insisted we ....

13 "I will meet you in front of the drugstore," he told us.

He told us ....

14 "We can repair the car today," he insisted.

He insisted they ....

15 "You can save money if you travel by bus," he suggested.

He suggested I ....

2 Proficiency check

a Look at the questions. Then listen to the recorded message about the festival and check (✔) the correct box for each one.

1 The Richmond Festival takes place from:
   a) August 7 to 30. ○
   b) August 17 to 13. ○
   c) August 17 to 30. ○
   d) August 7 to 13. ○

2 Which composer's work is being performed at the Kennedy Center on August 18?
   a) Beethoven ○
   b) Rossini ○
   c) Mozart ○
   d) Tchaikovsky ○

3 The Movie Society is showing movies from:
   a) Colombia, Brazil and Chile. ○
   b) Brazil, Paraguay and Mexico. ○
   c) Brazil, Mexico and Panama. ○
   d) Brazil, Mexico and Argentina. ○

4 Dr. Barbara Morrison is:
   a) giving a lecture on Shakespeare at Harvard University. ○
   b) giving two lectures in the Community College. ○
   c) acting in *A Midsummer Night's Dream.* ○
   d) a member of the Royal Shakespeare Company. ○

5 The jazz and blues concerts are every day:
   a) between 1:00 and 2:00 p.m. ○
   b) between 12:00 and 3:00 p.m. ○
   c) between 1:00 and 3:00 p.m. ○
   d) between 2:00 and 3:00 p.m. ○

6 You press 2 if you want:
   a) information about accommodations. ○
   b) to buy tickets. ○
   c) information about other events. ○
   d) information about excursions. ○

b Read the statements below about the soccer player, Diego Maradona. Then read the text and decide if they are correct (C) or incorrect (I).

1 Diego Maradona wrote his autobiography before he was 40. C ○ I ○
2 He was very poor when he was a boy. C ○ I ○
3 His father worked 11 hours a day. C ○ I ○
4 He became a professional soccer player when he was 16. C ○ I ○
5 In 1986 Argentina won the World Cup. C ○ I ○
6 He made a lot of money playing for big teams. C ○ I ○
7 He has had problems with alcohol. C ○ I ○

Diego Maradona is one of the world's most famous soccer players. Although he is only 40, he has just published his autobiography. One hundred and fifty thousand copies have been printed and will be sold in 80 countries. Maradona was born in the shanty town of Villa Fiorito in Argentina. He was one of eight children and the family lived in one room. He only had one pair of pants and his father worked from four in the morning until three in the afternoon.

Diego was such a talented soccer player he made his professional debut at the age of 15. He played for Argentina for the first time when he was 16, and by the age of 19 he had already scored 100 league goals. His first World Cup game in 1982 was a disappointment and he played badly. But in 1986 in Mexico he was part of the Argentina team which won the World Cup. In the game against England, he scored two goals: the first with his hand, and a fantastic second goal. Maradona said the first goal was "the hand of God."

Later he played for famous teams such as Barcelona and Naples and was one of the highest paid players in the world. Sadly, he has had problems with drugs which he hasn't been able to solve. However, in Argentina he is still a hero and people remember the poor boy from Villa Fiorito.

Unit 7 Trends

1 My generation

1 Speaking

a Work in pairs. When was this photograph taken? What clues are there?

b How are people from your generation different?

2 Listening and speaking

a Listen to Joanne Michaels talking about her life in the 1980s. Check (✔) the topics she mentions from the list.

1 music	3 politics	5 family	7 rock groups	9 events
2 clothes	4 movies	6 games	8 magazines	10 TV programs

b Listen again and complete the information about Joanne.

	Games	Music	TV programs	Movies	Clothes	Memorable events
Joanne	....	Duran Duran &	"Scooby Doo" &	.... & *Indiana Jones*	....	Challenger explosion & ....
You						

c Now complete the row for your generation and compare your choices with two other students.

3 Pronunciation: linking

a Listen to the examples of linking 1–4 below, and match the linked words to the descriptions a–d.

1 I was bor**n** **i**n 1967.
2 He's to**o** **o**ld to play soccer.
3 Are you French? Yes, **I** **a**m.
4 She's a membe**r** **o**f generation X.

a) /r/ to vowel
b) consonant to vowel
c) a 'back' vowel (as in *so, now, too*) is joined to another vowel by /w/
d) a 'front' vowel (as in *tea, be, see*) is joined to another vowel by /j/ (*Sh**e** **i**s French!*)

60

🎧 **b** **Work in pairs. Read sentences 1 and 2 and identify the type of linking (a, b, c or d from exercise 3a). Then listen and check your pronunciation.**

1 When I was a teenager I didn't have my own room.

2 This apple is absolutely delicious.

4 Reading, speaking and writing

a **Work in groups. Do you know the two groups shown above? What do you think are the main differences between them? Discuss your ideas.**

b **The texts below are from two newspaper articles about the two groups. Identify the three paragraphs that belong to each article and put them in the correct order. Check your ideas from exercise 4a with the texts.**

The Backstreet Boys: Paragraphs 1 ◯ 2 ◯ 3 ◯

The Corrs: Paragraphs 1 ◯ 2 ◯ 3 ◯

a) The vocal quintet sing a mixture of pop and Rhythm and Blues. Six months after forming they were one of Florida's hottest live acts and signed with Jive Records. In 1995, their second single *I'll Never Break Your Heart* was a huge success and in April 1996 they released their first full-length album.

b) Their first album *Forgiven, Not Forgotten* in 1995 was a mixture of traditional Irish music and pop. The group toured non-stop and lead singer Andrea appeared in the movie *Evita*.

c) One of Ireland's most successful pop exports of the 90s, the family group the Corrs consists of Jim on guitar and keyboards, sisters Sharon, violin and vocals, Caroline, drums and vocals and Andrea, lead vocalist. After forming in 1991, they played locally in Dublin and signed with Atlantic Records in 1994.

d) A very popular group, by 2001 they had sold 28 million albums worldwide and had scored five Top Ten singles. Their album *Millennium*, released in 1999, has sold over 10 million copies. *Black and Blue*, another album, released in 2001, will probably be just as successful.

e) The Backstreet Boys' incredible story began in Orlando, Florida in 1993. High school students A.J. McLean, Howie Dorough and Nick Carter met each other at local acting auditions and formed a singing group. The trio then decided to expand by two, adding Kevin Richardson and his cousin Brian Littrell.

f) The next album *Talk on Corners* was a more pop-oriented album and included several hot singles: *What Can I Do?* and *So Young*. The album eventually sold one million copies. Their third album *In Blue* was a hit and the single *Breathless* was an international success.

c **Read the articles again and complete the table below.**

d **Complete the final column of the table, writing about your favorite group or singer.**

	The Backstreet Boys	The Corrs	Your favorite group / singer
country of origin			
type of music			
name of latest album			
best-known songs			

2 Looking good

1 Word builder: clothing

a Look at the photograph and then match each article of clothing with the correct word from the list below.

baseball cap	jeans
tie	T-shirt
mini skirt	suit
sweater	sandals
leather jacket	boots
tank top	coat
pants	dress
hat	jacket
sneakers	anorak
blouse	shirt
socks	tights
shoes	

b Which clothing articles are not included in the photograph? Can you find examples of these words in your class?

c Work in pairs. Imagine you could each pick two items of clothing to wear. Which would you choose? Compare ideas with your partner.

2 Grammar builder: order of adjectives

a Look at the examples.

- *a blue cotton shirt*
- *a large khaki bag*

Based on these examples, decide the usual order for adjectives.

material ◯ color ◯ size ◯ + noun

Language assistant

Notice that opinion adjectives – great, nice, beautiful, ugly – come first:
*I got a **great** leather jacket.*

b Put these sentences in the correct order.

1 ugly / red / an / sweater / wool
2 large / a / brown / of / leather / boots / pair
3 gold / round / a / watch / small
4 plastic / black / long / raincoat / a

c Work in pairs. Look at what your partner is wearing for 30 seconds. Then sit back to back and describe your partner's clothes.

You're wearing a pair of black jeans, a blue wool sweater, ...

3 Speaking and reading

a In pairs, look at the photograph and make a list of at least five things you know about Barbie dolls.

Barbie dolls are sold all over the world.

TATTOO BARBIE GETS THE CHOP

Barbie dolls have been part of American culture since they were first sold in 1959. Aimed at 6 to 9-year-old girls, Mattel, the maker of Barbie, has sold more than one billion dolls worldwide. The Barbie range includes Malibu Barbie, Babysitter Barbie and Wedding Barbie. Every year a new Barbie arrives on the market.

However, anyone can make a mistake, as Mattel showed. The company introduced a version of Barbie which they said would be "every mother's nightmare." Butterfly Art Barbie came with a butterfly tattoo on its stomach and a set of temporary transfer tattoos for the owner. A Mattel spokesperson said: "Nowadays tattoos are classed as art."

Although the firm acknowledged that the new toy might inspire young girls to want a real tattoo, it argued it was only keeping up with fashion. The spokesperson said: "Ask any cool chick and she'll tell you that tattoos are one of the latest fashion crazes."

Mattel was right about one thing. Parents were outraged and the company took Butterfly Art Barbie off the market.

b Now read the article and mark the statements T (true) or F (false).

1 Barbie dolls have been sold for over 50 years.   T ○ F ○
2 Over a billion Barbies have been sold in North America.   T ○ F ○
3 Butterfly Art Barbie had a butterfly tattoo on its shoulder.   T ○ F ○
4 The company thought the doll would definitely make lots
   of girls want real tattoos.   T ○ F ○
5 The spokesperson for Mattel said that tattoos for girls are fashionable. T ○ F ○
6 Mattel withdrew Butterfly Art Barbie because parents were angry.   T ○ F ○

c Discuss these questions in groups of three.

1 Which of the following do you think are fashionable?
2 Would you personally have any of these?

| streaked or dyed hair | tattoos | studs in any part of the body | earrings for men | a woolen hat |

3 Shop till you drop

1 Word builder: shopping items

a Put the following list of items into one of these four categories.

1 men's toiletries   **2** makeup   **3** computers   **4** sports

razor blades	racket	monitor	tennis balls
mouse pad	aftershave	lipstick	face cream
deodorant	keyboard	baseball bat	running suit
eye shadow	shaving cream	laptop	mascara

b Work in groups of three. What are the six most important items in your everyday life? Talk about them in your groups.

2 Listening

a Listen to interviews with four shoppers, and write down the articles each person bought.

Name	Articles
Sandra	
Jim	
Tony	
Kate	

b Who do you think spent most, and least? Why?

3 Grammar builder: quantifiers

a Look at the words in the box below. What do they have in common?

a few	a little	many	much	a lot of	most
both	neither	all	none	half	

b Put the quantifiers from the box into the correct columns below. Be careful, in some cases like *a lot of* you can use a quantifier with both types of noun!

Countable nouns (*cars*)	Uncountable nouns (*sugar*)
many a lot of	much a lot of

c Write the quantifiers on the scale from 0% to 100%.

0% ————————————————————————————→ 100%

.....none.....   ....   .a lot of.   ....

....

....

d Complete sentences 1–7, below, with an appropriate quantifier.

1 .... children like candy.

2 My cousin and I were born in Hong Kong, but we .... live in Australia now.

3 Yes, I'm ambitious. I want to get a good job and make .... money.

4 Can you help me? It will only take .... minutes.

5 .... of the people in my class speak at least two languages.

6 .... of us can speak Mandarin Chinese.

7 Only 50% of the class passed the math test. Yes, only ....!

> **Language assistant**
>
> In affirmative sentences use *a lot (of)*. If the style is formal, use *many* or *much*.
>
> • *A lot (of)* and *Lots (of)* are basically the same.
>
> • Quantifiers always come before a noun, or a noun phrase:
>
> *Could I speak to you for **a few** <u>minutes</u>, please?*
>
> *Could **all** of <u>the parents who are waiting</u> speak to me later, please?*

4 Reading and speaking

a Answer the questionnaire and check the key. Compare your answers with two other students.

Are you a shopaholic?

1 You have a free Saturday morning. Would you rather:
  a) buy a plant for your apartment?
  b) go straight to the local shopping mall?
  c) read the newspaper?

2 A clothing store in the mall has a sale and is full of people. Would you:
  a) go in but only buy what you really need?
  b) rush in to look for bargains?
  c) find a nice quiet place for coffee?

3 One of your friends is getting married next weekend. Do you:
  a) try to use existing clothes and maybe buy one or two new items?
  b) go straight out to buy a new outfit?
  c) find something to wear in your closet?

4 You're in your local supermarket and notice the imported cookies have an offer of buy one package and get one free. Do you:
  a) buy one because it's a good offer?
  b) buy two packages and get two free ones?
  c) ignore it because cookies are fattening?

5 You have to buy a jacket for work. Do you:
  a) think about what you want and go to a couple of stores to compare prices?
  b) spend a happy morning trying on jackets in every clothes store you can find?
  c) go to the nearest clothes store and buy the first jacket that looks all right?

6 You feel really depressed. To feel better would you:
  a) go and have a coffee in your favorite coffee shop?
  b) go and buy something you really wanted?
  c) go to bed early with a good book?

Answer key:
Mostly As – You like shopping but you can control it most of the time.
Mostly Bs – You are a real shopaholic. You are never happier than when you are in a department store or mall.
Mostly Cs – Shopping isn't your cup of tea. You'd rather be doing anything else!

b Discuss the questionnaire with the class. Find out which of the statements 1–4 are T (true) or F (false).

1 Half of the class hates shopping. ◯

2 Most people think that clothes aren't important. ◯

3 A few people buy clothes every week. ◯

4 A lot of people shop in malls. ◯

LANGUAGE **for life:**

getting the *idea*

① Types of music

How much do you know about music? Can you recognize different types of music? Listen to the six different pieces of music and see if you can classify them correctly.

rock 'n' roll ◯   classical ◯   heavy metal ◯
jazz ◯   rap ◯   latin ◯

Can you match the names of the well-known people to the photographs / pictures above, and identify the type of music they are famous for?

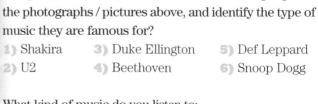

1) Shakira   3) Duke Ellington   5) Def Leppard
2) U2   4) Beethoven   6) Snoop Dogg

What kind of music do you listen to:
to relax?   to dance?   while you're working / studying?
first thing in the morning?   at parties?

② The Mozart effect

Read the article below and underline the points where they talk about the positive and negative effects of music. There are four points.

This week in our books section, we review *The Mozart Effect*.

"The nervous system is like a symphony orchestra with different rhythms, melodies and instruments," Don Campbell writes in *The Mozart Effect*. The title refers to studies showing that the music of Mozart can cause a temporary increase in IQ, but the book covers the entire range of effects music can have on us. Music is not just entertainment. It can be used to heal the body, strengthen the mind and unlock the creative spirit.

Music can also influence the early development of children. Studies have shown that children learn more at school and are likely to be nicer to each other if they are played pleasant, calming music such as Albinoni's Adagio in G minor. On the other hand, if they listen to exciting, aggressive music, their performance goes down and they become more antisocial.

③ Lyrics

How much can lyrics tell you about a song? Look at the excerpts from two songs shown here and answer the following questions.

1 What is the theme of each song?
2 What kind of music do you think goes with each song? (fast, slow, loud, soft, country and western, rock 'n' roll, blues, pop, etc.)
3 When do you think you would listen to each song?

Now listen to each excerpt and check your answers. Which excerpt do you like the best?

A

When I was young, it seemed that life was so wonderful
a miracle, oh it was beautiful, magical
And all the birds in the trees, well they'd be singing so happily
Joyfully, playfully watching me
But then they sent me away to teach me how to be sensible
Logical, responsible, practical
And they showed me a world where I could be so dependable
Clinical, intellectual, cynical
There are times when all the world's asleep
The questions run too deep
For such a simple man.
Won't you please, please tell me what we've learned
I know it sounds absurd
But please tell me who I am

The Logical Song – Supertramp

B

Yeah yeah yeah yeah yeah
Yeah yeah yeah yeah yeah
I think I did it again
I made you believe we're more than friends
Oh baby
It might seem like a crush
But it doesn't mean that I'm serious
'Cause to lose all my senses
That is just so typically me
Oh baby, baby
Oops! … I did it again
I played with your heart, got lost in the game
Oh baby, baby
Oops! … You think I'm in love
That I'm sent from above
I'm not that innocent

Oops! I did it again – Britney Spears

In pairs, look at the music magazine quiz below, and answer the questions.

Win a pair of free tickets to the Westlife concert. Just answer these questions and send them in:

1 **What's your favorite type of music?**

2 **What singer or group do you hate the most?**

3 **What's your all time favorite song?**

Finally, write in 20 words why you think music is important in life.

Unit 8 Big moments

1 Personal firsts

1 Speaking

Work in pairs and talk about what's happening in the photograph. Complete your sections of the table below, and interview another student to complete their sections. Use the examples to help you make up your questions.

When did you go to your first party?
What did you do there?

How did you feel the first time you went to a night club?

Who did you go to the night club with?

First	You When / who / what	You How you felt	Partner When / who / what	Partner How you felt
party / night club				
time driving a car				
day at school				
girlfriend / boyfriend				
money earned				

2 Listening

a Listen to two people talking about firsts and identify the topics they are talking about.

b Listen to the people talking again and answer the questions below. Check your answers in groups of three.

Steve

1 What was Jane like?
2 What was she really good at?
3 Why couldn't Steve talk to her?

Wendy

1 What was Wendy's job?
2 How much did she earn?
3 What didn't she like about the job?

c How did each of these people feel about their firsts?

3 Speaking and reading

a In pairs, look at the photograph and identify the sport. Has anyone you know ever done any extreme sports? Which? Would you like to do any of these sports? Why / why not?

b Read the text and identify the sport that is being described and the reason the person wanted to do it.

At the end of a party, when our minds weren't too clear, my friend Barry and I discovered we had both always wanted to jump out of an airplane. Before we had a chance to think about it, we'd checked the Yellow Pages, found a "drop zone," chosen a date and signed the "I accept I may die horribly" form. After a day's course the plane took off with four "first-timers" plus the jumpmaster Mick and the pilot.

When the plane reached three thousand five hundred feet we were ready to go. Mick shouted "in the door" and Barry sat in the open door with his legs hanging outside. Mick shouted "Go" and he jumped out and disappeared. Then it was my turn. I was apprehensive but not terrified. On the word "Go!" I threw myself out and spread my arms and legs and kept my eyes open as I shouted, "One thousand, two thousand, three thousand, four thousand check canopy!" Thankfully, the main parachute was open and I could relax and admire the view.

I landed perfectly near the drop zone but suddenly fell over and discovered I was dizzy. I waited for the world to stabilize and walked back to the airport.

The first thing I did was to buy two more jump tickets!

c Read the text again and put the following list of events in the right order.

1 When he jumped his parachute opened safely.
2 He landed safely but didn't feel completely well.
3 The writer and Barry took a day's course in parachuting.
4 Barry jumped out of the plane first.
5 He decided to do another parachute jump.
6 He jumped out of the plane and looked around him.
7 The writer and Barry found details about parachuting in the Yellow Pages.

4 Pronunciation: intonation – showing interest

a Listen to these two excerpts from the interviews in exercise 2. What do you notice about the intonation of the phrases in italics?

1 **Steve:** Her name was Jane and she was really cute.

Sonia: *Was she?*

2 **Wendy:** I used to ride about 4 miles a day.

Sonia: *Did you?*

b Work in pairs. Write a short question in the spaces, and practice reading it out loud.

1 **A:** I found $100 in the street.

   B: ....? Lucky you!

2 **A:** My first day at school was horrible.

   B: ....? Why?

c Change pairs and talk to another person about your firsts in exercise 1.

2 Your first date

1 Speaking and listening

a Look at the photographs above and guess what the two people are talking about. How are these people feeling? What do you think is the reason for the phone call?

b Listen to the conversation and check your ideas.

c Work in pairs. Read the conversation below and try to put it in the correct order. The first three have been done for you. Then listen again to check your answers.

Tania:	Oh, I remember. How are you?
Alan:	Oh wow! Is 7:30 OK? I can pick you up at your place.
Tania:	This is Tania speaking.
Alan:	See you Friday!
Tania:	Hmm, OK. Why not? What time?
Alan:	Oh, um, hi. Could I speak to Tania?
Tania:	On a date?
Alan:	Oh, hi Tania. It's Alan Turnsberry. We're in biology class together.
Tania:	Hello.
Alan:	Fine. Look. Um, I was wondering Tania, if … um, would you like to go out with me.
Tania:	Fine. Thanks for calling, Alan. Bye.
Alan:	Yes. How about Friday? We could have coffee or go bowling. Whatever you like.

(ordering circles: 3 at "This is Tania speaking.", 2 at "Oh, um, hi. Could I speak to Tania?", 1 at "Hello.")

2 Speaking and reading

a What are the important things to think about when you go on a first date? Work in groups of three and make a list of points for her and him.

b You are going to read some advice on what to do on a first date. Read the texts on the next page quickly to compare your ideas.

The Perfect Date

Her

You don't need to dress formally. To feel relaxed, choose something that's stylish but comfortable.

You have to get your hair done.

Wear some makeup and perfume.

Relax and have a good time.

Don't apply or reapply lipstick at the table.

Be pleasant to people around you, say "please" and "thank you" to waiters, etc.

Don't play with your hair.

When the bill comes, offer to pay. Hopefully, he will decline your generous offer.

At the end of the meal, excuse yourself to do your hair, makeup and check for food in your teeth in the ladies' room.

4

Him

Pick a place and call to make a reservation.

You have to take a shower and use a deodorant.

Put on some cologne.

Get your hair cut and wear clean clothes.

You don't have to take a present but some flowers or chocolates are a nice touch.

Tell her she looks lovely when you first see her.

Pay attention to her and introduce her to people you know.

Assume you are paying the bill. Don't let her pay on the first date.

If you can't afford a meal or movie, suggest going for coffee.

Before going, thank her for a lovely evening, even if it wasn't.

5

c Work in groups of three. How is this view of dating similar to and different from going out with people nowadays? How was dating in your parents' generation different from your generation?

3 Grammar builder: obligation and necessity

a Look at the following examples and answer these questions.

1 Which of the sentences talk about something being unnecessary?
2 Which sentences talk about obligations?

a) You don't need to dress formally.
b) You have to get your hair done.
c) You don't have to go to the meeting.
d) You must make a tax declaration every year.
e) You mustn't smoke in the building.

b Change these sentences if they are not true for you or your country.

1 I don't need to tell my parents if I'm coming home late.
2 We don't have to serve in the military.
3 You must carry an ID card at all times.
4 Boys have to help with housework.
5 You have to drink and drive.
6 I need to study every evening after class.
7 18-year-olds must ask their parents' permission if they want to marry.

c A foreign student is coming to your school or workplace for one term. Write a short paragraph explaining the main obligations and needs for people in your school or workplace.

You don't have to wear uniform. You mustn't smoke in the offices.

Language assistant

The opposite of *have to* is **not** *don't have to*. *Don't have to* means that you are free from obligation.

Do I **have to** *wear a suit at the wedding? No, you* **don't have to,** *but you can if you want to.*

- The opposite of *must / have to* is *mustn't*.
- Imperatives can be used as orders: *Don't touch that! It's hot!*
- Imperatives can also be suggestions: *Pay attention to her.*

3 The big day

1 Speaking and reading

a Look at the photographs above. Identify the occasions and talk about what is happening.

b Match the invitations below to three of the occasions in the photographs.

1

*Mr. and Mrs.
James Carmichael*

*have the pleasure of inviting you to the
wedding of their daughter,
Melanie, and Mr. Brian Stone*

At St. Mary's Church, Wallingford, Connecticut

On Saturday, June 24 at 3:00 p.m.

*Reception to follow at the
Four Seasons Hotel*

RSVP

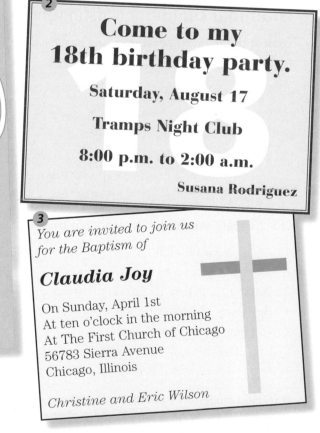

2

Come to my
18th birthday party.
Saturday, August 17
Tramps Night Club
8:00 p.m. to 2:00 a.m.

Susana Rodriguez

3

*You are invited to join us
for the Baptism of*

Claudia Joy

On Sunday, April 1st
At ten o'clock in the morning
At The First Church of Chicago
56783 Sierra Avenue
Chicago, Illinois

Christine and Eric Wilson

c Discuss the following questions in groups.

1 Which of these occasions have you experienced?
2 What are the best and worst occasions that you remember?

2 **Word builder:** weddings and graduations

a Which of the following words do you associate with weddings and which with graduations? Write them under the appropriate headings.

Weddings   **Graduations**

ceremony	examination	honeymoon	bride	champagne	college	bachelors	ring
reception	generation	groom	engagement	marry	graduate	best man	degree

b Can you think of any other words for these occasions? Write two more under each heading.

3 **Reading and listening**

a Look at the advertisement. What kind of a company is this and what do they organize for you?

b Listen to the conversation about wedding arrangements, and check (✔) the items on the advertisement that you hear mentioned.

WEDDINGS UNLIMITED
We help create beautiful wedding memories!
Let us make your special day more special.
50 years of experience count!

Audiovisual equipment   Balloons   Catering   Ceremony
Musicians   Churches   Disc jockeys   Flowers   Gifts
Hair salons   Invitations   Live bands   Limousines
Photographers   Transportation   Videographers

Contact us on tollfree 1-0800-387-4936 or e-mail us at
weddings@weddingsunlimited.com

4 **Grammar builder:** prepositions of time

a Look at the following examples. Notice the prepositions.

On Saturday, October 17.

*We'll go to the church **at** 2:30.*

*They're getting married **in** October.*

b Put the following list of dates, days and times in the appropriate column. When do we use *in, on* and *at*?

in	on	at

January	3 o'clock	Saturday morning	the afternoon	my birthday	Christmas
the weekend	the summer	Monday	5:50 p.m.	lunchtime	Independence Day
midnight	August 26	Easter			

c Complete the following questions with the correct preposition.

1 Where do you usually go .... Easter?
2 What do you usually do .... weekends?
3 What did you do .... your last birthday?
4 What were you doing .... 7:30 yesterday evening?
5 Do you have your longest vacation .... the summer
    or .... the winter?

d In pairs, ask and answer the questions in exercise 4c above.

LANGUAGE for life:

job *hunting*

1 Job hunting

Look at the job advertisement below and answer these questions.

1 Which of the qualifications or skills do you have?
2 Would this job interest you? Why? Why not?
3 What information about the company would you want before going to an interview for this job?
4 Where is the company located?
5 What would I take to the interview?
6 What should I wear?

Norton & Martin, one of the leaders in marketing, are recruiting a Personnel Manager.

Suitable candidates will have

● A college degree
● Advanced training in the area of personnel management
● Excellent PR skills
● 5 years' experience in personnel
● Preferably experience in the marketing area
● Computer skills

Competitive salary and benefits package.
Candidates should send a letter of application with details of current salary and a current résumé to Ms. T. Lopez at tlopez@norton&martin.com not later than Wednesday, October 19.

Listen to an expert talking about preparation for an interview. Complete the notes for each heading.

Company key information –

Common questions – Practice answers to common questions.

Rehearse interview with a friend –

Prepare interview material –

Clothes –

2 Résumés

OK, you've found a job you like. Now all you need to do is to send in your résumé. Let's look at a sample. Read the résumé and fill in the spaces with information from the box under it.

SAM RODRIGUEZ

1 Forest Road, Minneapolis MN 65743 .... e-mail: srodriguez@aol.com

Objective: A position in which my abilities, education and experience will be utilized to benefit the institution

Education: .... Harvard Business School 1998

B.A. in Economics. University of Minnesota 1996

Experience: Head of Operations, Pizza Express, 1998 – present; ....

Other skills: Word processing – ...., Excel, PowerPoint

Languages: Spanish (fluent), ...

.... Reading, ..., volunteer work for Greenpeace, tennis

References: Available on request

Write your own résumé and ask another student to check it for you.

French (reading and writing)   Tel: 612-876-546   Word 1999
Administrative Manager, Iceland Frozen Foods 1996–1998
Degree in Management   **Activities / interests:** cooking

③ Making a good impression

OK, you got the interview and the big day has come. How are you going to make a good impression? Share your ideas in groups and make notes on at least six ideas. Then look at our ideas and see if you are really ready for this interview.

They say that most interviewers make that all-important decision on who to employ in the first four minutes of an interview. So making a good impression is crucial. Follow these basic steps to guarantee a successful result on the day:

- Be on time. Being on time (or early) is usually interpreted as evidence of your commitment, dependability and professionalism.
- Be positive and try to make others feel comfortable. Show openness by greeting with a firm handshake and smile. Don't make negative comments about your current employer.
- Relax. Think of the interview as a conversation, not an interrogation.
- Be prepared. Take time to think about likely questions and answers. Think of key questions to ask.
- Show self-confidence. Make eye contact with the interviewer and answer his or her questions in a clear voice.
- Remember to listen. Communication is a two-way street. If you talk too much, you may miss important points made by the interviewer.
- Reflect before answering a difficult question. If you are unsure about how to answer a question, you might reply with another question.
- When it is your turn, ask the questions you prepared in advance.

- Show you want the job. Talk about things you could do that would benefit the organization. Don't ask questions that make the interviewer doubtful about you. Too many questions about vacations may make the interviewer think you are more interested in time off than helping the company.
- Dress conservatively but attractively. Wear a suit, clean shoes, a tie (for men), simple jewelry and moderate makeup (for women).
- Avoid negative body language: frequently touching your mouth, swinging your foot or leg, chewing your lip, folding your arms and avoiding eye contact.

4 Learning check

1 Progress check

a Read the text below and look carefully at each line. Some of the lines are correct and others have a word which should not be there. Check (✔) the correct lines or write the words which should not be there.

The modern fashion is a mixture of old and new ...... The ......

but it still influences what we decide to wear. .... ✔ ....

1 Many of young people wear bell bottoms and tops ....

2 which were fashionable in the late 1960s. ....

3 Today, both long skirts and tank tops were worn in the 1970s. ....

4 By choosing clothes we all choose the image we want to ....

5 project. But think before you throwing away any of your clothes. ....

6 They'll be fashionable again sooner or later. ....

b Complete the sentences using the correct preposition in each case.

7 They traveled to the coast .... their car.

8 Alex's birthday is .... October 13.

9 The party is .... Diana's house.

10 I have a week's vacation .... July.

11 The movie starts .... 8:30 p.m.

c Read the text. Complete the text with the correct words from the list below.

Before (**12**) .... exercise always warm up first. (**13**) .... warm-up you should stretch (**14**) .... your arms and legs and breathe deeply. Take at least 15 to 20 minutes before any energetic exercise. And remember, when you finish, take a few minutes to stretch your muscles. (**15**) .... of us should do regular exercise, but don't take any risks.

12 a)	do	b)	doing	c)	to do	d)	did
13 a)	To	b)	After	c)	On	d)	At
14 a)	many	b)	some	c)	both	d)	any
15 a)	Every	b)	No one	c)	Any	d)	All

2 Proficiency check

a Read questions 1–4, then listen to the conversation. Check (✔) the picture which best answers the question about each conversation.

1 Which musical are they going to see?
2 Which gift is the man going to buy?

3 What does Hazel look like?
4 What do they need to buy?

A ○   B ○   C ○   D ○   A ○   B ○   C ○   D ○

A ○   B ○   C ○   D ○   A ○   B ○   C ○   D ○

b Read sentences 1–4 and the text. Decide which sentence goes in each space (a–d).

1 Treatments relieve symptoms but do not correct the basic problems.
2 They protect us and repair the damage caused by disease.

3 This led to sanitation systems that protected people from the devastating infections that had habitually plagued mankind.
4 Many infectious diseases could finally be prevented or cured.

A revolution is sweeping through medicine. The first revolution occurred soon after British surgeon John Snow discovered, in 1854, that cholera is spread by contaminated water. (a) ....

The second revolution, surgery with anesthesia, came about at the same time, allowing doctors to fix ailments such as appendicitis and bowel obstruction. The third revolution was the introduction of vaccines and antibiotics. (b) ....

But, aside from attacking infectious diseases and some surgical problems, physicians do not actually "cure" anything. Medicines just help the body heal itself. (c) ....

Human genetic engineering – the fourth revolution – will profoundly change the practice of medicine over the next 30 to 40 years. Human genetic engineering is based on the premise that our genes are the defense and healing system of our body. (d) ....
Genes which function abnormally can contribute to cancer, heart disease, Alzheimer's and mental illness. Genes can be used to treat disease either by injecting more genes into patients or by modifying the function of the genes in the body.

Unit 9 Men and women

1 Evaluating tradition

1 Speaking

a In groups, discuss the following question.

Which of the jobs below do you think of as masculine (M)? Which as feminine (F)?

company director ◯   nurse ◯   librarian ◯   secretary (personal assistant) ◯
veterinarian ◯   pilot ◯   basketball player ◯   elementary school teacher ◯

b Continue in groups, and discuss the following questions.

1 Which jobs are more highly paid?
2 Is the percentage of men and women in traditional "male" or "female" jobs changing? Can you give some examples?

2 Listening, writing and speaking

🎧 **a** Listen to interviews with two couples. Which couple (A or B) is more traditional and which is more non-traditional?

🎧 **b** Listen again. Then write reasons why you consider each couple traditional or non-traditional.

1 Couple ……… is more traditional because …
2 Couple ……… is non-traditional because …

c Compare your notes with a partner.

3 Reading and speaking

a Read the information in the box. Do any of the facts surprise you? Why?

> **Some facts on equality of the sexes in the United States, in the past and now …**
>
> **1970:** Fifty-two percent of the population were female, but 2 percent of management jobs were held by women.
>
> **1975:** Married women were not allowed to have credit cards in their own names. Women earned an average of 40% less than men. Only 2 percent of business travelers were women.
>
> **1987–1999:** The number of businesses owned by women increased by 103%.
>
> **2000:** Almost 50% of business travelers were women, but women earned an average of 20% less than men. The majority of women in corporations were in low-level jobs.

b **In groups, discuss the answers to the following questions. Then read the article below and compare the information with your answers.**

1 When and where did the women's movement begin? Why did it begin?

2 In what areas were women asking for equal rights?

3 What were some of the arguments against the equal rights movement?

THE LONG ROAD TO EQUAL RIGHTS

"A woman without a man is like a fish without a bicycle,"
Gloria Steinem

When most people think of feminism, they think of the women's movement in the 1960s. But that was what women's rights groups refer to as "the second wave." The women's movement actually started around the beginning of the 20th century in the United States, Europe and Australia, when women began to enter the work force in great numbers. They felt that if women were going to work, they should have certain legal rights.

The second wave of the movement began in the mid-1960s when women began to demand equal rights in education, employment and legal issues. Women wrote books and articles on the subject, held conferences and organized protest marches with thousands of people to gain support for women's rights.

Opponents of the women's rights movement said that feminists didn't want to be women, that they wanted to destroy the family, as well as many other arguments. But in fact, the central idea of the feminist movement was very simple: Men and women are equally capable and therefore should be equal legally.

Since the 1960s, laws and attitudes in many countries have changed dramatically. But have they changed enough? In the United States, for example, the Equal Rights Amendment (a proposed addition to the U.S. Constitution) was first introduced in 1923. It says that equality of rights should not be denied on the basis of sex. This amendment still has not been approved and added to the Constitution.

4 Writing and speaking

a **In pairs, write as many arguments as you can, either for or against traditional roles for men and women (choose one).**

b **Now try to imagine the arguments of the opposing point of view. How will you answer them?**

c **Have a debate with a pair arguing the opposing point of view. If possible, have your debate in front of the class. The class will judge the winners!**

A: *I believe women shouldn't work because if they work, they don't have time to take care of the house or cook.*

B: *But if both work, they won't have to worry about money. They can share the housework and cooking so that one person doesn't have to do it all.*

2 Coincidence or destiny?

1 Reading and speaking

a Read the following story and underline all the coincidences you find. How many are there?

Michelle was flying from Houston to London, and during the flight, she began talking to John, the man in the seat next to her. She found out that he was president of a famous blue jeans company based in Texas; in fact, she was wearing a pair of jeans from his company! But that wasn't the most surprising thing. He had lived in San Francisco when he was in high school, and it turned out that he knew Michelle's best friend, who also grew up in San Francisco! They continued talking, and by the end of the flight, they felt that they had known each other for much longer than 8 hours.

But back in Houston, Michelle almost forgot about the attractive man she had met on the plane. One evening, she was walking her dog when a much larger dog came running toward them, growling. The owner was running after it, shouting. He managed to catch the dog just as it was going to attack Michelle's dog. Michelle was furious. "Why don't you keep your dog on a leash?" she yelled. Then suddenly, she looked at him and stopped yelling. "John?" "Michelle?" they said at the same time. Michelle said, "Do you live around here? I live on the next street." "I don't believe it," he said. "In a city of two million people, you live three blocks from me!" And in the end, as had to happen, Michelle and John began going out together – all because of seats on an airplane and a couple of dogs!

b In pairs, give the story a title which will make people want to read it.

c In groups, talk about coincidences that have happened in your lives.

2 Listening, reading and writing

a Listen to the conversation about a coincidence. What was the coincidence? Do the speakers believe in destiny? Do you believe in destiny?

b Read the e-mail that Patrick wrote to a friend, telling her about Steve's girlfriend. Rewrite it, correcting the factual errors. How many errors did you find?

◀ Back	▶ Forward	✕ Stop	🏠 Home	Print	Mail

Address:

Hi, Celia. How are you?
You remember Steve Berry, right? Well, he's convinced that he's been touched by destiny. He decided to take a painting class at the university, and he met his new girlfriend there. After the class, he was talking to the professor and she was standing next to him. They started talking about their families, and guess what. Her mother used to go out with his father when they were in school! Steve thinks that if he hadn't talked to the professor that day, he wouldn't have met her because it's a big class. Anyway – destiny or just coincidence – it's good news because Steve is IN LOVE for real. OK, no more gossip, so I'd better go do some work.
Write soon.
Love, Patrick

3 Grammar builder:
third conditional

a **Look at the two statements below and answer the questions.**

1 If Jeff had gotten up early, he wouldn't have missed the plane.
   a) Did Jeff get up early?
   b) Did he miss the plane?

2 If Mary hadn't taken a taxi, she would have been late to the meeting.
   a) Did Mary take a taxi?
   b) Was she late to the meeting?

b **We use the third conditional to imagine unreal situations in the past. Look at this example. How does the grammatical form change from a real to an unreal situation?**

*Jeff **didn't get up** early. He **missed** the plane.*

*If he **had gotten up** early, he **wouldn't have missed** it.*

c **Now change these real situations into unreal ones.**

1 Brandon grew up in Hawaii, so he learned to surf very well.

   If he hadn't grown up in Hawaii, he wouldn't have learned to surf.

2 Mark didn't tell me about the party, so I didn't go.
3 I wasn't good in science, so I didn't study medicine.
4 We arrived late at the conference, so we didn't hear the opening talk.

4 Pronunciation: sentence stress – conditionals

a **Listen to the following sentences and mark the stressed words in each clause. Which parts of the conditional structure are stressed in an affirmative clause? Which in a negative clause?**

*I would have **gone** to the **beach** if I **hadn't** had to **work**.*

1 We wouldn't have come if you hadn't called us.
2 If I had stayed in Florida, I would have seen the hurricane.
3 If you hadn't bought that car, you'd have some money.
4 Karen would have come to the movie if she hadn't had to work late.

b **Listen again and practice saying the sentences with correct intonation.**

5 Speaking

In groups, talk about events which have influenced your lives. How would your lives be different if the events had been different?

If I hadn't gone to Miami last year, I wouldn't have met my girlfriend. I met her at a party there.

If I had gotten married after high school, when my boyfriend wanted to, I wouldn't have gone to college. I'm glad I didn't get married!

3 Gifts of love

1 Speaking, listening and reading

a Read the song and discuss the questions.

1 Look quickly at the song below. What holiday is it associated with?

2 Do you celebrate this holiday? How?

3 Look at the song again. What is the topic?

🎧 **b Listen, and read the song.**

On the first day of Christmas, my true love sent to me
A partridge in a pear tree.
On the second day of Christmas, my true love sent to me
two turtle doves and a partridge in a pear tree.

Third day – three French hens
Fourth day – four calling birds
Fifth day – five golden rings
Sixth day – six geese a-laying
Seventh day – seven swans a-swimming
Eighth day – eight maids a-milking
Ninth day – nine lords a-leaping
Tenth day – ten ladies dancing
Eleventh day – eleven pipers piping
Twelfth day – twelve drummers drumming

c Now imagine that a modern-day boyfriend decided to give these gifts to his girlfriend.
Read her e-mails to him, shown below and opposite, and answer these questions.

1 How did Sarah feel on the first day?

2 Did she like the gifts on the second day?

3 By the fourth day, how did Sarah feel about Robert's gifts?

4 Why did she feel differently on the fifth day?

5 By the seventh day, how many birds had Robert sent in total? Figure it out!

6 By the ninth day, what types of gifts had Robert sent?

7 What was the subject of Sarah's e-mail on the eleventh day?

8 Who was the last letter from? Why?

DAY 1
Darling Robert,
Thank you for the beautiful
partridge in a pear tree.
Your love,
Sarah

DAY 2
Robert, the turtle doves
are lovely – and so is
the second partridge in
a pear tree. Kisses,
Sarah

DAY 4
Dear Robert, I don't know
what to say. The calling
birds and the French hens
are lovely, but please
don't send any more
birds! Love, Sarah

DAY 5
Oh, Robert - five gold rings! Now that's a nice gift! But I wish you hadn't sent more birds! I now have 5 partridges in pear trees, 8 turtle doves, 9 French hens and 8 calling birds!
Love, Sarah

DAY 7
Robert, is this a joke? It isn't funny! Geese and swans? And more partridges, etc.? I don't want any more birds!
Sarah

DAY 9
Robert, what is the matter with you? Now you're sending maids with cows, and lots of lords leaping all over the place! Do you know what it's like to clean up after all those cows and birds? Come and take all these "gifts" away!

DAY 11
Robert, I'm going to call my lawyer if you don't get these birds, cows, milkmaids and lords out of my house! And now pipers! I can't stand the noise! You're crazy - I wish I had never met you!

January 15th
Dear Mr. Lowell,
This is to inform you of a lawsuit filed by Ms. Sarah Garver for damages to her property and mental health. She claims you have sent to her house 12 partridges in pear trees, 22 turtle doves, 30 French hens, 36 calling birds, 40 gold rings (she'll keep those), 42 geese, 42 swans, 40 milkmaids and cows, 36 leaping lords, 30 dancing ladies, 22 pipers and 12 drummers.
Ms. Garver is currently in the Sunny Day Psychiatric Hospital.
Martin Landau, Attorney at Law

2 Grammar builder: *wish*

a **Look at the first example of a wish in the table below.**

1 Did the person lead a healthy life? Is he happy about the life he led?
2 What verb tense is used after *wish* to talk about past unreal situations?
3 Find more examples of wishes in the e-mails in exercise 1c. What did the boyfriend do that Sarah didn't like in each case?

b **Complete the table with your own ideas. Then discuss them with your classmates.**

Wish about an unreal situation	Who said it	Real situation
I wish I had led a healthier life.	I think an old, ill person said it.	The person didn't lead a healthy life.
I wish my movies had been more famous.		
I wish our team had practiced more!		
I wish my boyfriend hadn't done that!		

3 Speaking

In groups, talk about things you wish you had or hadn't done in the past.
Ideas: opportunities for work or study, relationships, money, etc.

I wish I had studied business instead of biology. There are more job opportunities in business.

LANGUAGE for life:
business and social *customs*

① From culture to culture

When you deal with people from other cultures, it is helpful if you have learned something about the customs and attitudes of those cultures. For example, attitudes about men's and women's roles vary greatly from one culture to another. Consider the questions below.

1 What is sexism? Is it a positive or negative concept?
2 Does the concept of sexism exist in your culture?

🎧 Now listen to some short conversations and choose the correct answers to the questions below. Pay attention to the actual words of the conversations.

Conversation 1
1 What does the woman want to do?
2 Who is the guest?

Conversation 2
1 Where does the man plan to take the woman?
2 How does he describe the event?

Conversation 3
1 What does the first man give his guest?
2 What does the second man say about it?

Conversation 4
1 What does the man offer to do?
2 Whose car are they going to use?

🎧 In the previous exercise, you focused on facts. Now listen again and pay attention to tones of voice and intonation.

Conversation 1
How does the woman feel?
a) She's a little insulted.
b) She's happy that the man will pay.

Conversation 2
What does the woman mean?
a) She doesn't know what a bullfight is.
b) She isn't sure she wants to see a bullfight.

Conversation 3
What can we infer?
a) The man doesn't really like the drink.
b) He likes it a lot.

Conversation 4
What does the woman mean?
a) She wants to drive.
b) She wants the man to drive.

Learning tip

Listening comprehension is not only understanding the words people say. It is also sometimes understanding what they **don't** say! People use devices like stress and intonation and pauses as well as words to communicate their attitudes and opinions. So learn to "listen between the lines!"

Say how you decided on the answers to the questions above.

② The culture of international business

In groups, imagine you are on an international flight. Read and discuss the in-flight magazine quiz below. Which actions would you consider most appropriate? Which least appropriate? There are no "right" answers, but give reasons for your choices.

THE ANGLO-AMERICAN BUSINESS CULTURE QUIZ

Imagine that two business colleagues (a man from Britain and a woman from the United States) are coming to your country, and they have been there several times before.

1 You have made a schedule for your colleagues' stay in your country.
  a) You call them on the phone to tell them personally about the activities you've planned.
  b) You send them an e-mail with the complete schedule, including social activities.
  c) You wait and give them the schedule personally when they arrive.

2 The visitors arrive at 8:00 p.m.
  a) You meet them at the airport.
  b) You send a driver from the company to meet them.
  c) You send them instructions for taking airport transportation to their hotel.

3 They will be in your city for the weekend, and you want to provide them with some entertainment.
  a) You decide to take the man to a bullfight. Your wife will take the woman shopping.
  b) You and your wife take them both to an arts and crafts fair and to a restaurant for lunch.
  c) You give them some suggestions for things to do and how to get there. You will see them on Monday.

4 One evening the man feels ill. You (a man) had planned to take your guests to dinner. You ...
  a) cancel the dinner because the man can't go.
  b) take the female visitor to dinner but invite your wife so there are no "misunderstandings."
  c) go to dinner with your female colleague.

5 A female executive from your office has a business lunch with the visitors at a restaurant.
  a) She pays the bill.
  b) The male visitor pays the bill.
  c) Everyone pays his or her share.

③ Planning for visitors

You've now read quite a lot about the attitudes and customs of English-speaking business people. Imagine that you are planning weekend entertainment for a foreign colleague visiting your city. Write an e-mail message suggesting a plan. Ask him or her to tell you which of the suggested activities he or she would prefer.

Exchange e-mails with a partner. Now imagine you are the visitor. Read your partner's e-mail and write an answer. Say which activities you would prefer and give reasons. Be polite!

Unit 10 Life's a journey

1 Stranger than fiction

1 Speaking and reading

a You are going to read a true story. Before you read, look at the photographs below. What do you think the story is about?

b Now read the newspaper story. Did you guess the topic of the story?

c Choose the best headline.

1 Patricia Hearst to go to prison for terrorist activities
2 Hearst family unhappy about conviction
3 Patty Hearst renounces support for SLA

Patricia Hearst, granddaughter of media king William Randolph Hearst, was convicted today of armed robbery for her cooperation with her terrorist-kidnapers in the robbery of a San Francisco bank several months ago. Though she has given up her support for the terrorist group, she will go to prison for her participation in the robbery.

Hearst was kidnaped several months ago from her Berkeley apartment when unidentified gunmen took her from the apartment and forced her into the trunk of a car.

Several days after she was kidnaped, her kidnapers contacted the Hearst family. They called themselves the Symbionese Liberation Army and demanded that the Hearsts use their fortune to help poor people. The Hearsts agreed to sponsor a food giveaway program.

After several weeks in captivity, Patty Hearst announced that she was in sympathy with her SLA captors. She said that she was renouncing her family's wealth and upper-class lifestyle and that she was changing her name to "Tania." As Tania, she was involved with the SLA in the bank robbery. Security cameras showed that she was not merely a victim, but an active participant in the robbery. Finally, police received a tip about the SLA's hiding place in Los Angeles. There was a shootout in which some SLA members were killed. Hearst and other members escaped to San Francisco, where they were caught a few days later.

d Look back at the first paragraph of the newspaper article about Patty Hearst. Complete the table below.

Who:	
What:	Hearst sentenced to go to prison
Where:	
When:	
Why:	

2 Speaking, writing and reading

a Imagine you are a magazine writer. You are going to write an article about what happened to Patricia Hearst after her prison sentence. Complete the table with the main ideas of your first paragraph. Use your imagination!

Who:	
What:	
Where:	
When:	

b Write the first paragraph of your story, and write a headline for the story.

c In groups, read your paragraphs. Whose story was the most interesting? Whose was the most probable? Write the rest of your story.

d Read the end of the Patty Hearst story, below. Were there any similarities with your story?

Despite her family's wealth and importance, Patricia Hearst went to prison for armed robbery. During her prison term, she finished her college studies, and when she left prison, she returned home to live with her family. She finally married her bodyguard, and today she has a family of her own.

Why did Patty become Tania in 1974?

Some psychologists said she must have been brainwashed by her captors. Others said she might have felt guilty about her family's enormous wealth in a time of radical social change in the United States. In the end, only Patty knows the reasons for "Tania."

2 A near tragedy

1 Speaking and listening

a Discuss the following questions.

1 What could happen on a mountain climbing expedition?

2 Why do you think mountain climbers take risks?

3 Do you know of any disaster stories about mountain climbers?

b Listen to the first part of the interview about an unsuccessful mountain climbing attempt. Write down the three mistakes mentioned.

c Listen to the second part of the interview. What does Chris say his group should have done? What shouldn't they have done? What could have happened? Check (✔) the boxes below.

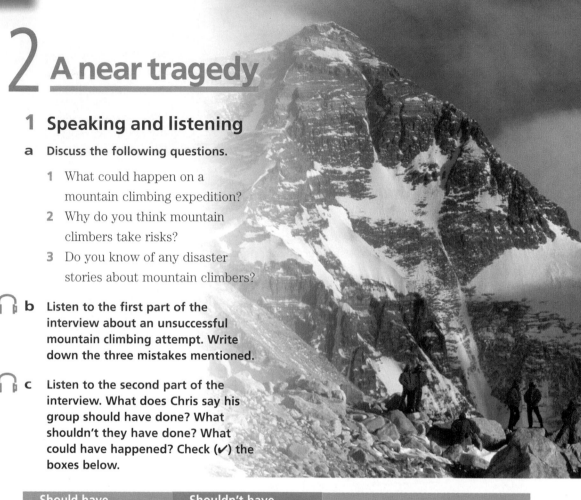

Should have ...	Shouldn't have ...	
		checked the weather
		gone in March
		gone in May
		continued after the snow started
		taken Gary with them

2 Grammar builder: past modals – *would have*, *should have*, *could have*

a Look at sentences 1–3, below, from the interview in exercise 1. Match them with their meanings, a–c.

1 We should have gone down the mountain immediately. ....

2 He could have died. ....

3 It would have been our fault for taking him with us! ....

a) an unreal condition in the past (It wasn't the case because the action didn't happen.)

b) a recommendation about a past action (It was the right thing to do, but they didn't do it.)

c) a possibility in the past (It was possible, but it didn't happen.)

Language assistant: past modals

subject	+ modal	+ present perfect
Gary	could	have died.

b **Read the following story and answer the questions below.**

Derek was buying a newspaper in a small store when a man entered the store with a gun. He told the clerk to give him all the store's money. Derek ran up behind the man and hit his arm, knocking the gun out of his hand. The gun fired, but fortunately, no one was injured. The thief ran out through the door and escaped.

1 What did Derek do? In your opinion, should he have done this? If not, what should he have done?

2 What could have happened?

3 What would you have done if you had been there?

3 Pronunciation: weak forms – modals

a **Listen to two people talking about Derek's experience. Circle the past modals you hear.**

A: Did you hear what happened to Derek?

B: Yeah, I *would have / wouldn't have* been terrified!

A: Me too. I *would have / wouldn't have* attacked the man! Derek *could have / couldn't have* been killed!

B: He *should have / shouldn't have* hit the man. He *should have / shouldn't have* called the police.

b **Listen again and practice the sentences. Notice the reduced forms.**

/wouldev/   /wouldnev/   /shouldev/   /shouldnev/   /couldev/   /couldnev/

4 Writing and speaking

a **In pairs, comment on the following situations.**

1 Marty was riding his motorcycle when a car turned in front of him. He fell off his motorcycle, but fortunately he wasn't hurt. He wasn't wearing a helmet.

2 Karen went to a movie with one of her brother's friends. She didn't tell her boyfriend because she thought he might get angry.

3 Sam and Joe were accused of robbing a convenience store last Saturday. The police didn't believe their story that they were at a party, even though witnesses said they saw them there.

b **Think of a difficult or dangerous situation in your past, or invent one.**

1 Write a short description of what happened.

2 Write a few sentences about what you should or shouldn't have done, and what could have happened.

c **In groups, read your stories. Say what you would have done, or how you would have felt in a similar situation.**

3 War of the Worlds

1 Listening and reading

a Listen to excerpts from a radio broadcast from 1938. Then check (✔) the correct answers to the following questions.

1 What type of radio program does it sound like?

a) news ◯   b) drama ◯   c) music ◯

2 What was the topic of the broadcast?

a) a fire in New Jersey ◯   b) explosions in space ◯   c) the arrival of aliens on earth ◯

3 How does the announcer sound?

a) amused ◯   b) terrified ◯   c) angry ◯

b Now read the following article about the effects of the radio broadcast and answer these questions.

1 What kind of program was *The War of the Worlds*?

2 What did many people think when they heard the broadcast?

3 What was the general result?

4 What were three reasons why people thought the broadcast was real?

On This Day in History

The Orson Welles Effect

On the night of October 30, 1938, CBS's New York radio station WABC broadcast Orson Welles' dramatic version of *The War of the Worlds*, a novel by H.G. Wells. The work was introduced as a play, and three times during the broadcast, the station announced that it was fictional.

Nevertheless, it sounded like a news broadcast, and a lot of people thought that the earth was being invaded by Martians! Mass panic resulted. Thousands of people began calling newspapers and radio stations for information about the "end of the world." Because part of the radio program had recommended evacuation, many families left their homes, trying to escape the New York–New Jersey area.

Many people reacted to the panic in ways which today seem very amusing. In Newark, New Jersey, some families ran into the street with wet towels over their faces because they thought there was a Martian gas attack. The *New York Times* received 875 calls from frantic citizens. One man called to ask, "What time will the end of the world be?" When a bus station employee tried to question a caller about the situation, the caller said she didn't have time to talk because "the world is coming to an end and I have a lot to do."

What could have caused so many people to believe that Martians were attacking the earth? Psychologists say that it might have been partly because of the world political climate. Europe was

heading toward World War II and there was a general feeling of insecurity. Another factor was the broadcast itself. It was extremely realistic and in the form of news bulletins. It must have sounded like the real thing to a lot of people. Finally, many listeners missed the beginning of the program, when it was explained that they were going to hear a radio play.

c What would you have thought if you had heard *The War of the Worlds*?

2 Grammar builder: past modals – *could have*, *might / may have*, *must have*

a The above modals are used to make deductions about the past. Look at sentences 1–7, below, and write the modals in the correct places in this table.

a definite conclusion (99% sure)	a possibility (50% sure)	an impossibility (99% sure)
	might (not) have	

1 Some people might have panicked because of other people, not because of the broadcast.

2 Others might not have heard the beginning of the program.

3 The panic could have happened partly because of political insecurity.

4 Some people may have seen airplane lights and thought they were spaceships.

5 The radio station may not have made it clear that it was fiction.

6 The people who thought Martians were invading must have been terrified.

7 Welles couldn't have imagined that his drama would cause such panic.

Language assistant

- *Could, may* and *might* have approximately the same meaning.
- The opposite of *must have* for deductions is *could not have* and **not** *must not have*!

Derek **must have** been scared.
Derek **couldn't have** been an accomplice in the attempted robbery.

In spoken form, *must have* and *might / may have* are not usually contracted in the negative.
Have is reduced: He *must / might / may not've known.*

b Complete the conversation with appropriate past modals.

A: Did you hear about that actress who killed her husband?

B: Yeah, she (1) .... (*kill*) him for his money. I'm sure that was the reason.

A: No, she (2) .... (*want*) more money. She has millions!

B: True. Well, then, she (3) .... (*be*) jealous. He (4) .... (*have*) a girlfriend.

A: Yeah, she (5) .... (*find out*) he was in love with another woman.

B: Yep, that (6) .... (*be*) it. I mean, it's always money or love, right?

3 Speaking

a In groups, think of a famous myth or legend from your country. Summarize it. Does everyone in the group know the same version?

b Myths and legends must have come from somewhere! Try to think of reasons for the origin of yours. Use the examples to help you describe your reasons.

There must have been a murder ...

A woman may have lost her child ...

There could have been a tribal war, and ...

La Llorona

91

LANGUAGE for life:
making the most of *travel*

① Ready to travel

Imagine you're getting ready to go to Britain. In pairs, make a list of things you've heard, read or imagine to be true about it.

Discuss your list with the class. How many of the things may be stereotypes and not necessarily completely true?

In groups, discuss the following questions.

1 What do you think you need to know before you go on a trip?
2 How can you find the information you need?
3 What can you do during your visit to learn more about the place than the "average" tourist?

② Learning from travel

Read the following article from a travel guide and compare it with your ideas from the exercise above.

THE ABOVE-AVERAGE TRAVELER

The right attitude

Most countries, or even regions, have certain stereotypes connected with them – Americans eat fast food all the time and have little family life. New Yorkers are all loud and unfriendly, etc. But anyone who has traveled a lot will tell you that stereotypes are exactly that – stereotypes, and don't represent the broad spectrum of customs and attitudes which exist in every country or region.

Before you go

If you are planning a trip, how can you prepare so that you benefit as much as possible from the experience? First, learn some basic facts about the place – its capital, the basis of its economy, a little of its history, its main ethnic groups, etc. You can get an overview from a travel guide, an encyclopedia or the Internet. The Internet also has specific information about cities – maps, restaurant recommendations, etc.

If you're going to another country, try to take a basic survival course in the language. If you already speak the language, a conversation class can increase your fluency. Reading newspapers or magazines from the country will

increase your vocabulary and will also give you information on important current events there.

Whenever possible, talk to people from the country you're going to visit. You can often meet people through a language institute or college in your city. Internet chat rooms are another way to talk to people from other countries and find out their ideas and attitudes about things.

When you get there

Once you get to your destination, how can you avoid being "a typical tourist"? Of course, it helps if you know someone there. They can show you lots of great places tourists don't usually go. But if you don't know anyone, there are still a

number of things you can do to learn as much as possible about the country. First, try not to stay in a "tourist hotel." Bed and breakfasts are a good option because they're often owned by families and much more personal than a hotel.

Don't eat hotel food, or what you imagine to be the typical food of the country (hamburgers in the United States or pasta in Italy). Ask about local specialties – barbecue in Texas or Cajun food in New Orleans, for example. And don't use a tourist guide for restaurant recommendations. Ask local people where they eat, or ask a taxi driver to take you to his favorite restaurant.

Try to do things that local people do; again, don't just refer to your tourist guide. Ask people for suggestions or check the entertainment section of the local newspaper. And finally, talk to as many different people as possible. Most people are friendly to tourists and are happy to answer questions about their city.

Use your own ideas and ideas from the text to prepare for a visit to another country.

1 In groups, choose a country or a region in your own country.

2 Write a plan for learning as much as you can about the country or region before you go and after you get there.

3 Share your ideas with the class.

③ What kind of traveler are you?

Think of a trip you have taken and write a short composition about it.

Paragraph 1: What you did to prepare for the trip.

Paragraph 2: What you did while you were there.

Paragraph 3: What you should have done differently, or how you might have benefited more from the trip.

Exchange compositions with a partner. Read your partner's composition and comment on it.

I think I would have tried to meet some people. You could have learned more about local customs that way.

5 Learning check

1 Progress check

a Complete the second sentence of each pair so that it has a similar meaning to the first sentence of the pair.

1 I didn't get up early, so I didn't catch the bus.

If I had gotten up early, ... the bus.

2 He took the medicine and felt better.

If he .... , he wouldn't have felt better.

3 She didn't buy the dress because she didn't have enough money.

She .... if she'd had enough money.

4 I sold my car but it was a bad idea.

I wish .... sold my car.

5 Jane jumped down the stairs and broke her arm.

If she hadn't jumped down the stairs, ...

b Read the sentences and choose the correct completion for each space.

6 You .... put a band aid on that cut. It might get infected.

    a) might have   **b)** should   **c)** should have   **d)** would have

7 Our car crashed but we were very lucky. We .... been badly hurt.

    a) must have   **b)** should   **c)** had   **d)** could have

8 If I had known you didn't have any money, I .... you some.

    a) would have lent   **b)** should have lent   **c)** must have lent   **d)** would lend

9 I can't find my keys anywhere. I .... them at work.

    a) would have left   **b)** might have left   **c)** had left   **d)** will leave

10 The hotel had no heat. It .... really cold in your room.

    a) would have been   **b)** had been   **c)** could have been   **d)** must have been

c Replace the underlined words in these sentences with the correct form of one of the phrasal verbs in the box.

find out   turn down   go out with   get over   give up

11 Teresa <u>refused</u> the job offer because she doesn't want to move to Chicago.

12 I took tennis classes for six months but it was so difficult that I finally <u>stopped trying</u>.

13 We <u>discovered</u> that Jenny lives in the same street as us.

14 Luke has been off work for two weeks but he still hasn't <u>recovered from</u> his illness.

15 Sarah has been <u>dating</u> Liam for over three years.

2 Proficiency check

a Read the five statements. Then listen to the conversation and decide if the statements are correct or incorrect. Check (✔) YES for correct and NO for incorrect.

		YES	NO
1	Philip has a stomachache.	○	○
2	He has taken something for the problem.	○	○
3	He has had the problem for two weeks.	○	○

		YES	NO
4	He's going to the local hospital for an appointment.	○	○
5	Christine thinks Dr. Barnes isn't very nice.	○	○

b Match the headings in the list with the paragraphs of the article. There is one extra heading.

1 Home sweet home
2 Flower crazy
3 Childhood and early career
4 Concert tours
5 Financial affairs
6 Best-known songs
7 Clothes and accessories

a)

Elton John, whose original name was Reginald Dwight, was born in Pinner near London in 1947. As a child he learned the piano and began his career as a professional musician in 1965, playing the piano and singing with the group Bluesology.

b)

His first hit single was "Your Song" in 1971 and he established a reputation for melodious, sentimental ballads. One famous album was "Goodbye Yellow Brick Road" which included one of his most famous songs, "Candle In the Wind." This song was about the life of the actress Marilyn Monroe. He has also written music for movies such as *The Lion King*.

c)

Elton John is famous for his flamboyant stage costumes and glasses. He also has thousands of pairs of shoes as well as expensive jewelry. He has hundreds of Versace shirts with his initials. He has so many clothes, he has just opened a store in London to sell some of his thousands of outfits to benefit charity.

d)

Elton John has an insatiable appetite for luxury. He paid $7 million for a French castle in 1997. He spent the same amount again on furnishings and decoration. He also has a house near Windsor, a six-bedroom apartment in London and a condominium in Atlanta, Georgia.

e)

He has an obsession with fresh flowers. Two florists prepare 240 arrangements a week for his homes. In a 20-month period he spent $425,000 on flowers. During the same period, he spent $58,000,000 in total.

f)

He tore up financial reports without reading them and refused to see his accountants when they flew to Los Angeles to discuss a "serious financial crisis." "I have a flair for writing songs. I have a flair for performing and making records. I have never had an aptitude for business," he told reporters.

Unit 11 Stages of life

1 Learning to be human

1 Speaking and listening

a Look at the four photographs. In pairs, decide:

- approximately how old each child is;
- what they probably can and cannot do at that age.

b Jean Piaget (1896–1980) was a very influential developmental psychologist. He identified four main stages in the cognitive development of children. Listen to a college class about Piaget's theory, and complete the table below.

> "Pre-operational" stage   "Formal operational" stage
>
> "Sensori-motor" stage   "Concrete-operational" stage

Piaget's stages	Approximate ages
1 Sensori-motor stage	From birth to age ....
2	From age 2 to age ....
3	From age 7 to age ....
4	From age .... on

c Listen again and note some of the things children can do at each stage. Compare and discuss your notes in groups.

2 Writing, reading and speaking

a On a clean sheet of paper write a paragraph about a typical day in the life of a child you know well. Don't mention the age of the child.

b In groups, read one another's paragraphs. After reading each paragraph, note on the paper your name and the approximate age that you estimate for the child.

c Get your own paragraphs back. Who has made the best guess of each child's age? Then discuss the children, and see how well they match Piaget's stages of development.

3 Word builder: people

a Write the words from the box on the appropriate lines. You should write some words on more than one line. Use a dictionary if you need to.

baby	boy
girl	guy
grown-up	infant
kid	man
teenager	youngster
youth	woman

Child: ....

Adolescent: ....

Adult: ....

b Classify the words in the table by putting a check (✔) in the appropriate columns.

- Masc. (always masculine), Fem. (always feminine), or M/F (masculine or feminine)
- Inf. (usually informal), Form. (usually formal), or I/F (informal or formal)

	Masc.	Fem.	M/F	Inf.	Form.	I/F
SINGULAR						
1 guy						
2 child						
3 kid						
4 adolescent						
5 teenager						
6 youth						
7 mom						
PLURAL						
1 sons						
2 children						
3 parents						
4 fathers						
5 brothers						
6 siblings						

Learning tip

It is useful to keep a vocabulary notebook and write points like those above beside words: *brothers* (males only – for males and females *brothers and sisters*) The usefulness of this is not just that you can review words in the notebook, but the act of making the note helps you remember. What would you write for *parents* and *children*?

4 Reading and speaking

Read the extract from an anthropology thesis. In pairs, discuss the information in the paragraph. Consider questions like these.

1 Why are human babies born early?

2 What are the advantages of our long dependence on our parents?

3 What else makes human children different from other young mammals?

Human children develop very differently from other mammals. Our childhood is proportionally much longer, extended at both ends, with early birth and late maturity. If the pregnancy period of human mothers were the same as other mammals in proportion to average body weight it would be more than a year, not nine months. However, at one year the human child's head would be too big for natural birth. One thing that makes us human is, literally, our big heads, which grow a lot more than other mammals' heads after birth. On the other hand, we do not become mature adolescents until we are much older than other mammals. We spend a much longer time depending on our parents. Therefore, we learn much more from them, and that accustoms us to continue learning all our lives.

2 Goals in life – or just wanna have fun?

1 Reading, writing and speaking

a Read what four 20-year-olds think about their lives. Which corresponds to each photograph?

1 "I'm just a year away from graduating. I already work part-time, and hope to get a good full-time job in the company once I graduate. But I have plans for bigger things – an MBA as soon as possible, and I'll be managing a department in the company when I'm 30."

2 "Although I'm studying, I don't expect to graduate. My fiancé already has a good job, and we're getting married next month. I'll be taking care of a baby by the end of next year, I hope. My real ambition is to be a good wife and mother."

3 "My grandaddy says 'You're only young once', and he's the happiest old guy I know. I reckon that's 'cos he really had fun when he was young, and I'm following his example. I'm studying too, but I don't plan to get serious about work until I'm, say, 10 years older."

4 "I feel so fortunate. We young people can have such full lives nowadays. I try to take advantage of every opportunity – self-development, preparation for a career, fun with friends, travel. But I suppose my real passion is biology, my major. I want to go into research."

b In pairs, discuss which person you identify with most, and least. Why?

c Write a paragraph about what interests you most at the moment: study, work, sports, having fun with friends, marriage, travel, etc. In groups, exchange and discuss your paragraphs.

2 Grammar builder: future progressive vs. future simple

a Look at the following sentences. Which ones are about:
- a complete, defined activity in the future?
- an open-ended activity taking place at a certain time in the future?

1   I'll be managing a department in the company when I'm 30.
2   I'll get an MBA as soon as possible.
3   I'll be taking care of a baby by the end of next year.
4   My mother will take care of the baby tonight, so we can go out.

b   **What is the difference in the verb structures in sentences 1–4 above?**

c   **Complete the sentences with the more appropriate structure: future progressive or future simple.**

1   We .... (*wait*) for you at seven o'clock. Don't be late.
2   They .... (*paint*) the house while we are away. They can finish in that time.
3   I .... (*pay*) them when we get back.
4   In ten years' time we .... (*live*) in a bigger house with a nice yard, I hope.
5   I .... (*work*) when you arrive, so wait for me in the café across from my office.

> **Language assistant**
>
> The future progressive is sometimes used for pre-arranged definite future activities.
>
> **I'll be seeing** Joan tomorrow.
> **I'll be taking** some wine to the party.
>
> This is most common when something is definitely going to happen or has been decided.
>
> **I'll take** some wine to the party would be a spontaneous decision rather than an arrangement, and so the future simple is used.

3   Pronunciation: linking

a   **How do you normally pronounce the underlined words below? Listen and check.**

1   My <u>mother'll</u> take care of little Bess tonight.
2   <u>What'll</u> she do if she cries?
3   <u>Bess'll</u> sleep like a baby. She always does.

b   **In pairs, ask and answer these questions.**

1   What time / go to bed tonight?
2   What / have for breakfast tomorrow?
3   How much / study next weekend?

4   Speaking

a   **Complete this table with your expected situations in five and ten years' time.**

	Five years' time	Ten years' time
Work and / or study		
Place of residence / type of accommodations		
Marital status / family life / social life		
Other activities / aspects of your way of life		

b   **In pairs, discuss and compare your lives in five and ten years' time.**

3 When I'm 64

1 Speaking

In pairs, talk about two elderly people you know.

1 How old are they?
2 Do they still work?
3 Do they live alone?
4 What are their interests and activities?

2 Reading and speaking

a Look at the picture and the title of the article below and discuss what you think it's about.

b Match the two parts of the following sentences from the article.

1 She will never return to the United States,
2 She didn't have very much money,
3 She got a job teaching English there
4 She was 64 years old when her husband died,
5 Although she had never been abroad before,

a) but she was still very young at heart.
b) she knew about Latin America from reading.
c) so she had decided to travel by bus, not by plane.
d) because she had taught English in high school.
e) unless there is some big family emergency.

c Read the article below and put the sentences you have completed in the appropriate spaces.

A HIGH OLD LIFE

Margaret Drysdale is American, but she lives in Cuzco, Peru. Ten years ago she lived in Kansas City, and had never been out of the United States. Then her husband died.

Her two married daughters wanted her to stay in Kansas City and be a grandmother to their children. However, she was not happy with that idea. (1)
....
Jack had never wanted to travel far from home, but Margaret had traveled through books, and now she wanted to really travel.

She told her daughters she would be going on a long trip soon, but they didn't believe her. She sold the house and moved into a hotel. They still didn't believe her. One winter morning she checked out of the hotel and took a taxi to the Greyhound terminal. (2)
....
She took the first bus south to the Mexican border.

She had been considering where to travel, and had decided to go all the way to Argentina and Chile. (3)
....
It attracted her more than anywhere else in the world.

She spent a year zig-zagging through Mexico and Central America, then Colombia and Ecuador to Peru. She was aware of a few dangerous situations, and quite unaware of several others. In Peru she began to worry about her diminishing funds. She started looking for some kind of work in Cuzco, high in the Andes, a city that fascinated her. (4)
....
Margaret has lived there happily ever since.

Her daughters have never visited her. They occasionally write or telephone, trying to persuade her to come "home." They don't realize that Cuzco is Margaret's spiritual home. (5)
....

d **Answer these questions.**

1 How old is Margaret Drysdale now?
2 How old was she when she left the United States?
3 Why did she leave?
4 What was her first year away like?
5 Why does she live in Cuzco now?
6 Would you do something like Margaret?

3 Grammar builder: connectors

a **Complete sentences 1–9, below, with connectors from the box.**

although	because	but	however	if	only if	so	therefore	unless

1 She did not have much money, ... she wanted to travel.

2 .... she did not have much money, she wanted to travel.

3 She did not have much money. ...., she wanted to travel.

4 She did not have much money, ... she decided to travel by bus.

5 She decided to travel by bus .... she did not have much money.

6 She did not have much money. ...., she decided to travel by bus.

7 She will return to the United States .... there is a family emergency.

8 .... there is not a family emergency she will not return to the United States.

9 She will not return to the United States .... there is a family emergency.

b **The sentences that you have completed in each group (1–3, 4–6, 7–9) have essentially the same meaning. In pairs, complete the related sets of connectors below.**

1 although, ..., ...
2 because, ..., ...
3 if, ..., ...

c **Write more sets of sentences like this one.**

Grandpa is old, but he is healthy.
Although grandpa is old, he is healthy.
Grandpa is old. However, he is healthy.

Language assistant

However and *Therefore* are common only in fairly formal writing.

4 Listening and speaking

a **Listen to an old man talking about himself, and complete the notes below.**

Name: ....
Age: ....
Reasons why he lives where he does: ....
Interests: ....

b **In groups, discuss the general situation of old people in your country.**

LANGUAGE for life:

scholarships

① Life after graduation

José Riveira is 22 and has just graduated, with a major in biology. For a little while at least, he can say goodbye to full-time study, term papers, and examinations – as well as all those fun times with fellow undergraduates. He has considered three main options for the next year or so of his life: a one-year trip bumming around Europe with three "hippie" friends, a job as an assistant in a local agricultural research institute, or a Master's program in the United States beginning in three months' time.

- *Which option would you choose, and why?*
- *Are you in a similar situation to José, or is your situation very different? What are your immediate plans or options?*

Well, José chose to go for a Master's, and he started investigating schools, costs and scholarships. Washington State University seemed interesting, partly because he has an uncle and aunt in Seattle. But the cost! (And W.S.U. is not expensive by U.S. standards.) How do the following figures for the 2000–2001 academic year compare with colleges in your country?

Tuition and Fees:	$13,850.00
Room and Board:	$5,276.00
Books:	$750.00
Health Insurance:	$435.00
Student Health Service Fee:	$136.00
Miscellaneous:	$1,923.00
TOTAL:	$22,370.00

② Getting a post-graduate scholarship

Obviously, José needed a scholarship, and with his good grades, he had a fair chance of getting one.

1 Have you or has anyone you know ever applied for or received a scholarship for study in the United States?

2 If so, what was the procedure, and how did it work out?

Most countries have scholarship systems for their residents to do post-graduate study abroad, but they usually work in conjunction with scholarship systems of the countries where the study will be carried out, for example, the U.S. Commission for Educational and Cultural Exchange. Procedures for application to the college selected (in José's case W.S.U.) and the scholarship bodies vary, but the latter usually requires the information in the form on page 103.

1 Many people hate filling out forms, so why not practice with this one?

2 Check with a partner.

FULL NAME
Last .... First .... Middle ....
SEX Male ☐ Female ☐
COUNTRY OF BIRTH ....
COUNTRY OF CITIZENSHIP ....
CURRENT MAILING ADDRESS
Street .... City .... State or Province ....
Zip code .... Country ....
Telephone .... E-mail ....
HAVE YOU EVER APPLIED TO THIS ORGANIZATION FOR A SCHOLARSHIP BEFORE?
No ☐ Yes ☐ Date: Month .... Year ....
WHICH U.S. UNIVERSITY ARE YOU APPLYING TO? ....
FOR WHICH COURSE OF STUDY? ....
HAVE YOU TAKEN THE TOEFL EXAMINATION?
Yes ☐ Date: Month .... Year .... Score ....
No ☐ Are you a non-native speaker of English? No ☐ Yes ☐
When are you going to take TOEFL? Month .... Year ....

EDUCATIONAL BACKGROUND

College or University	Location	Dates of study		Degree or diploma
1	....	From	to	....
2	....	From	to	....
3	....	From	to	....

HOW WOULD THE COURSE OF STUDY CONTRIBUTE TO YOUR CAREER OBJECTIVES?
....
....
....

The interview

Scholarship applicants are usually required to have an interview. With a partner, write a list of questions you anticipate you would be asked in such an interview.

🎧 Listen to part of a scholarship interview and note what the candidate, José, says about:

1 his specific interest in Washington State University;

2 the subject he is interested in, and his reason;

3 his English;

4 his reason for going directly from an undergraduate degree to a Master's degree.

🎧 Listen to the interview again. Modify the list of questions you wrote previously if you wish. Then practice an interview with your partner. Get ready to go for a scholarship / promotion / new job yourself! You can do it! Even if you're unlucky this time, you'll have learned something just from trying.

Unit 12 Crystal ball

1 Looking back at 2001

1 Reading

You are going to read an article about a science fiction movie called *2001: A Space Odyssey*. Read the quiz items. Then scan the article below the quiz to find the answers as quickly as possible. The winner is the person who finds all the correct answers first!

1 The movie was made in the:
   a) 1960s.   b) 1970s.   c) 1980s.

2 It was directed by:
   a) Robert Altman.   b) Steven Spielberg.   c) Stanley Kubrick.

3 The name of the space ship was:
   a) Discovery.   b) Voyager.   c) Explorer.

4 The computer in the movie was called:
   a) SAM.   b) HAL.   c) ED.

5 The computer had the ability to:
   a) see, hear and talk.   b) make decisions.   c) both a) and b) plus form opinions and feel emotions.

6 The computer was disconnected because:
   a) it started to make mistakes.   b) it began to kill people.   c) it used too much power.

7 When the computer was disconnected, it:
   a) quoted a poem.   b) sang a song.   c) made a prediction.

2001, Past and Present

In the late 1960s, the 21st century still seemed a long way in the future. Computers were just beginning to have widespread applications, and people did not have personal computers in their homes. However, some people were beginning to imagine, and sometimes to fear, the central role that computers would take in our lives in the future.

Director Stanley Kubrick's 1968 movie *2001: A Space Odyssey* was not a typical sci-fi movie about wars with space aliens. It had much more complicated and sophisticated themes, one of which was the role of machines in human lives. In Kubrick's vision of 2001, computers had assumed many human capabilities, which would lead to a fight for dominance between man and machine.

The setting of the movie is the space ship Discovery, which travels to different galaxies. The ship is entirely controlled and operated by a computer called HAL 9000. Kubrick's futuristic computer could see, hear and speak like a human. It was able to process all types of information and use it as a basis to make decisions. Finally, it formed opinions and felt emotions as humans do.

During the mission, HAL decides that the humans on the Discovery will not carry out the mission properly, and it (he?) begins to kill the members of the crew. Finally, the remaining crew members decide that HAL must be disconnected, and the struggle between man and machine begins. In the end, man triumphs and the computer is disconnected in a strange and emotional scene. As HAL's circuits are gradually shut down, his "mental" faculties diminish, paralleling what sometimes happens to the human brain. The once brilliant HAL ends up singing a very simple song over and over, more and more slowly, until at last there is silence.

2 Listening and speaking

a Listen to a conversation between a computer and its user, and answer questions 1–4, below.

1 Does the computer sound as human as the man?

2 How does the computer feel?

3 What arguments does the computer use to avoid being disconnected?

4 How did the scene make you feel?

b In groups, discuss the following questions.

1 Have you seen any science fiction movies? Which ones? Has anyone in the group seen *2001*?

2 Do you think science fiction can actually give us a preview of life in the future? Why or why not?

3 In your opinion, could computers ever become as "human" as HAL in *2001*?

3 Speaking and writing

a Stanley Kubrick commissioned several companies to predict what they might be selling in the year 2001, and to design the objects. Which description matches the object in the picture? Are any of the objects described below similar to things which now exist?

1 Picture Phone by Bell Telephone
   Bell actually made a set of these, and Kubrick used them to call his daughter.

2 Attaché case by Honeywell
   They predicted micro-technology.

3 "Robo Pen" by Parker
   A voice-operated pen with buttons to control handwriting, margins, ink color and language.

4 Charge card identifier
   Automatically checked the owner and the credit status of the card.

b In pairs, design an object on paper which you think people will be using 30 years from now. Write a description of the object and how it will be used.

c Present your invention to the class.

Today we would like to present the "X" to you. The "X" will …

2 Tomorrow's world

1 Speaking

a In pairs, decide which of the following things have been achieved.

Technology	Medicine	Ecology
instant information access	a vaccine against polio	electric automobiles
banking from home	a cure for cancer	protection of endangered species
voice-operated automobiles	artificial organ implants	alternative energy sources

b Compare your list with another pair. Which of the things do you think will be achieved or perfected in your lifetime?

2 Reading and speaking

a Scan the text below quickly. Which of the things in the list in exercise 1a are mentioned?

Centuries of Change

The 19th century was the era of industrialization, and the 20th century was the era of communications technology. The invention of the television in 1926 started a revolution in communications which would change the world. And by the end of the century, advanced computer technology meant that people could send and receive information instantly via the Internet.

The 20th century also saw major advances in other areas. For example, in medicine, antibiotics and a vaccine for polio were developed. Organs were successfully transplanted, and in some cases artificial organs were implanted. There were also advances in ecology. A number of international organizations now work to protect endangered species and to clean up and protect the environment. Alternative energy sources like wind and solar power were developed.

But at the beginning of the 21st century, an enormous amount of work is still needed to protect the earth and its inhabitants. By the end of the 21st century, what will we have achieved? Will we have cleaned up the air and water of our planet? Will plants and animals be safe from human destruction? Will we have achieved total sexual and racial equality? Will we have stopped fighting wars? It's difficult to imagine such a perfect world – but in the 19th century it was difficult to imagine machines that could count!

b In groups, discuss the questions in the last paragraph of the text above. Give reasons for your opinions. Which of the questions apply to your country? What other problems need to be solved?

3 Grammar builder: future perfect

a Look at the example. Which of the sentences 1–3, below, means the same thing as the example?

In 30 years, we will have found a cure for cancer.

1   It took 30 years, but we now have a cure for cancer.
2   Thirty years from now, we will find a cure.
3   We will find a cure sometime in the next 30 years.

b In the following text, circle the correct form of the verb.

Sometimes I think about how the world (1) *changes / will change* in my lifetime. I'm 30, and I (2) *have seen / will have seen* a lot of changes. For example, 15 years ago, people (3) *didn't know / hadn't known* how the Internet would affect everything! So what (4) *has happened / will happen* in the next 30 years? Well, I think we (5) *have stopped / will have stopped* using gasoline, and we (6) *drive / will drive* electric cars. In 10 years, we (7) *are inventing / will have invented* new energy sources. By the time I'm 60, we (8) *will solve / will have solved* a lot of problems!

> **Language assistant**
>
> The future perfect is for actions which will happen at or by a specific time in the future.
>
> *In two years, I **will have graduated** from the college.*
>
> *By 2006, I **will have been married** for five years.*

4 Listening and speaking

a Listen to the conversation about the future. In the table below, mark the predictions the woman believes with W, the ones the man believes with M, and the ones they both believe with B.

Predictions for the world in the year 2020	The conversation	Your opinions
1 Children will study at home, by computer.		
2 Computer transactions will have replaced money.		
3 Medical advances won't have increased people's life spans.		
4 We'll get all music, movies and books from the Internet.		
5 We won't have colonized space.		

b Now mark the sentences Y (yes) or N (no) according to your opinions.

c In groups, discuss your opinions. Write two more predictions about the world in 20 years and share them with your class.

3 Your future

1 Grammar review: future forms

a Look at the picture and read the conversation below quickly. What is the conversation about?

Frank: So, Ed, when do you finish school?

Ed: (1) ....

Frank: Great! (2) .... right away.

Ed: Uh, not exactly, sir. I think I'll probably do some traveling.

Frank: Ah, excellent. Check out job opportunities in other cities, right?

Ed: Uh, no, not really. When I graduate, (3) .... (4) .... , so I'd like to take a break first.

Frank: Oh, I see. Well, a short break is probably a good idea. (5) .... , I guess.

Ed: No, sir. In September I will have just started my trip. I plan to take a year to backpack from Toronto to Buenos Aires.

Frank: Oh! Well, it's not what we did in my day. Still, you'll be seeing a lot of different places and things on your trip. (6) .... , I'm sure.

b Now complete the conversation with the phrases below.

a) You'll be looking for a job in the fall then

b) I will have been in school for 19 years

c) I'll be working for the rest of my life

d) I graduate in June, sir

e) It will be very educational

f) I suppose you'll want to get a job

c Find an example of each of the following meanings in the conversation above.

1 a prediction

2 a definite, scheduled event in the future

3 an action which will be completed at a point in the future

4 an action which will be in progress at some point in the future

2 Pronunciation: intonation and emotion

a People use intonation to express emotions like surprise, anger, etc. This is true in all languages, but the way it is done varies between languages. Listen to these excerpts from the conversation. In each case, check (✔) how the people feel.

1 a) excited ◯   b) embarrassed ◯   c) angry ◯
2 a) unconvinced ◯   b) convinced ◯   c) angry ◯

3 a) happy   ◯   b) surprised   ◯   c) embarrassed   ◯

4 a) enthusiastic ◯   b) bored   ◯   c) embarrassed   ◯

5 a) surprised   ◯   b) disappointed   ◯   c) enthusiastic   ◯

b **Now practice saying the following sentences as indicated.**

1 I'm going to a conference. (excited)   4 Mary went out with Joe.   (angry)

2 I'm going to a conference. (bored)   5 I've forgotten your name. (surprised)

3 Mary went out with Joe.   (happy)   6 I've forgotten your name. (embarrassed)

3 Reading and speaking

a **Read the following profile. With a partner, make predictions about the person's future.**

1 Will he graduate from college?

2 Will he become successful?

3 What will he be doing in five years?

This young man is 19 years old, a student at the University of Texas. He is an expert with computers and enjoys anything related to computer technology. However, he doesn't like being a college student very much. As a freshman (a first-year student), he has to take many required courses like English and history which have nothing to do with computers. He feels that maybe a college education is not for him.

b **The profile you read was of a real person. Read what happened to the young man and compare his story with your predictions.**

During his freshman year in college in 1983, the young man began to buy excess inventories of RAM chips and IBM disk drives from local computer dealers. He then resold them for much less than retail prices by advertising in the newspaper. By 1984, his sales were averaging $80,000 per month! He decided to quit college and start his own company. Today that company is Dell Computer Corporation, and Michael Dell, college dropout, is on his way to becoming one of the richest people in the world!

4 Writing and speaking

a **Write a paragraph about your hopes and predictions for your future. Use the questions to help you.**

1 Where do you think you will be in 10 years?

2 What do you think you'll be doing?

3 What are some of the things you want to have done by then?

b **In groups, talk about your predictions and see if the others agree with you.**

LANGUAGE for life:
the world of *English*

①
The game of English

This is the last unit in the book, so it's time to stop working so hard and have some fun! Play the game opposite in groups and find out how much you know about English and the English-speaking world.

INSTRUCTIONS

1 Play in groups of 4–6.

2 You need a dice, and each player needs a coin or something similar to use as a marker.

3 One student in the group is the monitor. He or she looks at the answers below.

4 Each student rolls the dice, and the highest number goes first. Continue in order around the circle.

5 When it's your turn, roll the dice and move your marker the number of spaces indicated.

6 Answer the question on that space. If the answer is correct, stay on the space. If it's incorrect, return to your previous space. The monitor should not say the correct answer.

7 The first person to arrive at FINISH wins.

②
Roundup

In groups, or as a class, discuss your experiences with English so far.

1 In what ways have you been able to apply your knowledge of English?
2 Have you had any really enjoyable experiences using English?
3 What kinds of things do you now feel you can do reasonably competently in English?
4 How do you think you will be using English in the future?

Answers: 1 a, 2 c, 3 b,
4 a, 5 c, 6 a, 7 c, 8 c, 9 a,
10 b, 11 c, 12 c, 13 b,
14 b, 15 a, 16 a,
17 b, 18 b, 19 c, 20 b.

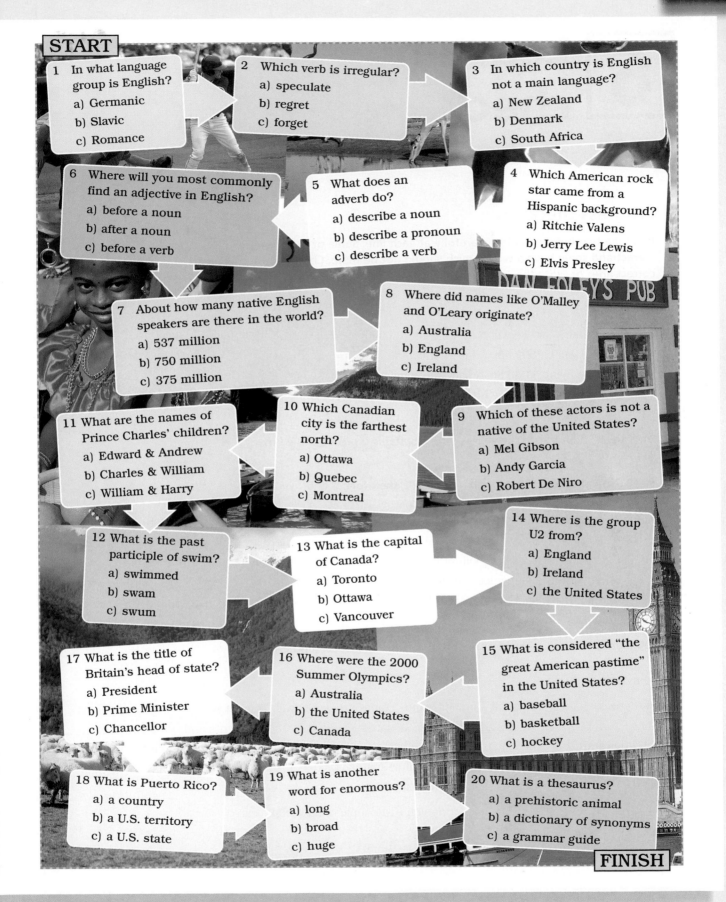

START

1 In what language group is English?
   a) Germanic
   b) Slavic
   c) Romance

2 Which verb is irregular?
   a) speculate
   b) regret
   c) forget

3 In which country is English not a main language?
   a) New Zealand
   b) Denmark
   c) South Africa

6 Where will you most commonly find an adjective in English?
   a) before a noun
   b) after a noun
   c) before a verb

5 What does an adverb do?
   a) describe a noun
   b) describe a pronoun
   c) describe a verb

4 Which American rock star came from a Hispanic background?
   a) Ritchie Valens
   b) Jerry Lee Lewis
   c) Elvis Presley

7 About how many native English speakers are there in the world?
   a) 537 million
   b) 750 million
   c) 375 million

8 Where did names like O'Malley and O'Leary originate?
   a) Australia
   b) England
   c) Ireland

11 What are the names of Prince Charles' children?
   a) Edward & Andrew
   b) Charles & William
   c) William & Harry

10 Which Canadian city is the farthest north?
   a) Ottawa
   b) Quebec
   c) Montreal

9 Which of these actors is not a native of the United States?
   a) Mel Gibson
   b) Andy Garcia
   c) Robert De Niro

12 What is the past participle of swim?
   a) swimmed
   b) swam
   c) swum

13 What is the capital of Canada?
   a) Toronto
   b) Ottawa
   c) Vancouver

14 Where is the group U2 from?
   a) England
   b) Ireland
   c) the United States

17 What is the title of Britain's head of state?
   a) President
   b) Prime Minister
   c) Chancellor

16 Where were the 2000 Summer Olympics?
   a) Australia
   b) the United States
   c) Canada

15 What is considered "the great American pastime" in the United States?
   a) baseball
   b) basketball
   c) hockey

18 What is Puerto Rico?
   a) a country
   b) a U.S. territory
   c) a U.S. state

19 What is another word for enormous?
   a) long
   b) broad
   c) huge

20 What is a thesaurus?
   a) a prehistoric animal
   b) a dictionary of synonyms
   c) a grammar guide

FINISH

6 Learning check

1 Progress check

a Read the text below and look carefully at each line. Some of the lines are correct and some have a word which should not be there. Check (✔) the correct lines or write the words which should not be there.

In the year 2025 the world population will be reach 8.5 billion.	...... be ......
61% of these people will live in cities.	...... ✔ ......
1 By the same year, we will have be sent 30 billion e-mails	....
2 and there will be 80 million Internet users.	....
3 We will be flying 3,000 billion air traffic miles a year.	....
4 Life expectancy will have be increased to 72.5 years.	....
5 The number of households headed by women will increase to 55%.	....

b Read the text and fill in the spaces with a suitable word from the box. There is one extra word.

if   so   because   although   unless   therefore   and

Many more people can now work from home (**6**) .... technology has made it unnecessary to go to an office. (**7**) .... more people work at home, there are fewer vehicles on the road. (**8**) ...., there is less pollution. (**9**) .... self-employment has increased, most people still work for companies, the government and institutions, (**10**) .... they still have to travel to and from work every day. (**11**) .... governments find ways to reduce the time and distance people travel to work, vehicles will continue to pollute cities everywhere.

c Complete the letter with the correct form of the verbs in parentheses.

Dear Mom and Dad,

Hi there. Well, here we are at summer camp. Things are going well. Tonight we
(**12**) .... (*go*) to a party to meet all the other students and tomorrow the
activities start. Caroline (my friend) and I (**13**) .... (*take*) a sailing course.
On Tuesday there's a trip to Charleston. Unfortunately, the bus (**14**) ....
(*leave*) at 5:30 in the morning. Can you believe it?

I (**15**) .... (*call*) you in a couple of days. Take care.

Love,

Amy

2 Proficiency check

a Listen to five people talking about their favorite TV programs. Match the subjects with the speakers. There is one extra subject.

Speaker 1 ◯   a) documentaries and wildlife   Speaker 4 ◯   d) movies
Speaker 2 ◯   b) sports   Speaker 5 ◯   e) news
Speaker 3 ◯   c) soap operas   f) comedy shows

b Read the article. Then, for each question, choose a, b, c or d and check (✔) the one you decide is correct.

Perhaps the most well-known sea mystery is that of the *Marie Celeste,* the "ghost ship" which was found drifting off the Azores on December 3, 1872. Ten days earlier the ship had left New York with Genoa, Italy as its final destination. On board the ship were Captain Benjamin Spooner Briggs, his wife and small daughter and an experienced crew of seven.

At 3 p.m. on December 3, the *Dei Gratia* found the *Marie Celeste* floating in the middle of the Atlantic Ocean. No one responded to the shouts from the crew of the *Dei Gratia.* Eventually, some sailors from the *Dei Gratia* boarded the *Marie Celeste* and for an hour searched the boat for any sign of life. There was none.

Below decks, things were very strange. A meal had been prepared in the kitchen. In the crew's quarters clothes lay on bunks and laundry was hung on lines. In one cabin was a chart showing the ship's position on November 24. In the captain's cabin there was a sewing machine and some toys.

More interesting was the fact that some items were missing from the ship: the sextant, chronometer, navigation book – and the ship's small boat. Why did the crew abandon the ship? There was no sign of damage to the ship or other factors, which could have explained why the crew left. No one could answer this question.

Although she was recovered and went to sea again, the *Marie Celeste* had an unhappy history. Over the next 11 years she was sold 17 times. She was thought to be unlucky and had a series of accidents before running aground in Haiti on a day with the clearest visibility.

1 The *Marie Celeste:*
   a) was traveling to New York from Genoa. ◯
   b) was found very near Italy. ◯
   c) was on its way from New York to Genoa. ◯
   d) sank near New York. ◯

2 The crew from the *Dei Gratia:*
   a) first saw the *Marie Celeste* early in the morning. ◯
   b) immediately decided to go and search the *Marie Celeste.* ◯
   c) weren't interested in the *Marie Celeste.* ◯
   d) went to search the ship after trying to attract attention. ◯

3 Inside the ship:
   a) a meal had been served on the table. ◯
   b) the crew's clothes were on the floor. ◯
   c) there was a map showing the ship's position earlier. ◯
   d) there was a washing machine. ◯

4 The missing things from the ship:
   a) were probably stolen. ◯
   b) were probably used for navigation. ◯
   c) were thrown into the sea. ◯
   d) were hidden somewhere on the ship. ◯

5 After the *Marie Celeste* was found:
   a) she was never used again. ◯
   b) she ran aground on her first voyage. ◯
   c) she was bought and sold many times. ◯
   d) she was a popular ship with sailors. ◯

Songsheet 1
Tears in heaven

1 Vocabulary work

Look at the words in the box. Then look at the words in context. In pairs, try to understand the meanings from the example sentences, without using your dictionaries, and then discuss the questions together.

1 to beg	2 to belong to someone	3 beyond

1 **to beg**: *Sometimes, people who need money beg from people on the street. And sometimes, teenagers beg their parents to let them stay out late.*

- If you see someone begging, do you always, sometimes or never give the person money?
- Have you ever begged your parents for permission to do something? Did they usually say yes?

2 **to belong to someone**: *You can't take the cassette player home because it belongs to the school!*

- How many things in this room belong to you?

3 **beyond**: *We heard a strange noise in the distance, beyond the far wall of the school. Business has changed beyond recognition since the introduction of the Internet.*

- Can you think of three other things that have changed beyond recognition over the last ten years?

2 Reading, speaking and listening

a Read these different ideas of what heaven may be like. Are any of them like your idea of heaven? Discuss your ideas together.

> "For me, heaven is a place of complete peace. There's no conflict and everyone is satisfied with what they have."

> "I see heaven as a place where I can be together with all the people who have been separated from me for whatever reason."

> "What I think of when I see the word 'heaven' is a beautiful place. All of the ugly things about the world have been removed and what's left is the fundamental beauty that I think you can find at the heart of everything."

> "My idea of heaven is a place of perfect understanding. Ignorance and confusion have no place there."

b Listen to the song and try to answer these questions.

1 Who is the singer speaking to?
2 Why do you think he can't stay in heaven?
3 What is his idea of heaven?

c Now look at the lyrics of the song and fill in the missing words.

Then listen to the song again and check the answers.

Tears in heaven

Would you know my (1) ....
If I saw you in heaven
Would it be the (2) ....
If I saw you in heaven
I must be (3) .... and carry on
'Cause I know I don't (4) ....
Here in heaven

Would you hold my (5) ....
If I saw you in heaven
Would you help me (6) ....
If I saw you in heaven
I'll find my way (7) .... night and day
'Cause I know I just can't (8) ....
Here in heaven

Time can bring you down
Time can bend your (9) ....
Time can break your (10) ....
Have you beggin' please
Beggin' please

Beyond the (11) ....
There's peace I'm sure
And I know there'll be no (12) ....
Tears in heaven

Repeat 1

3 Speaking

a Imagine you could spend one day in heaven! What would you do?
Who would you see?   What would you ask them?

b Now discuss your ideas in groups.

Songsheet 2
California dreamin'

1 Speaking

How much do you know about the U.S.? In groups, see how many of these questions you can answer.

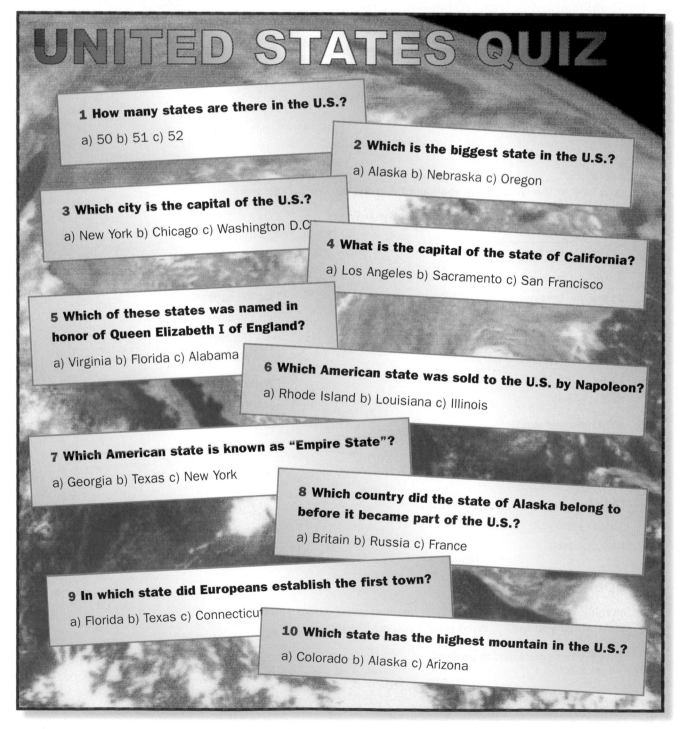

UNITED STATES QUIZ

1 How many states are there in the U.S.?

a) 50 b) 51 c) 52

2 Which is the biggest state in the U.S.?

a) Alaska b) Nebraska c) Oregon

3 Which city is the capital of the U.S.?

a) New York b) Chicago c) Washington D.C

4 What is the capital of the state of California?

a) Los Angeles b) Sacramento c) San Francisco

5 Which of these states was named in honor of Queen Elizabeth I of England?

a) Virginia b) Florida c) Alabama

6 Which American state was sold to the U.S. by Napoleon?

a) Rhode Island b) Louisiana c) Illinois

7 Which American state is known as "Empire State"?

a) Georgia b) Texas c) New York

8 Which country did the state of Alaska belong to before it became part of the U.S.?

a) Britain b) Russia c) France

9 In which state did Europeans establish the first town?

a) Florida b) Texas c) Connecticut

10 Which state has the highest mountain in the U.S.?

a) Colorado b) Alaska c) Arizona

2 Speaking and listening

a In pairs, look at the words of the song and the pictures. Try to replace the pictures with words.

California dreamin'

All the .... are brown
And the .... is gray
I've been for a ....
On a .... day
I'd be safe and ....
If I was in L.A.

California ....
On such a winter's day

Stopped into a ....
I passed along the way
Well, I got down on my ....
And I pretend to ....

You know the .... likes the cold
He knows I'm gonna stay
California ....
On such a winter's day

All the .... are brown
And the .... is gray
I've been for a ....
On a .... day
If I didn't tell her
I could leave today

California ....
On such a winter's day

b Now listen to the song and check your answers.

c Listen to the song again and answer these questions.

1 What season is it?
2 Why does the singer want to go back to California?
3 Why can't he go back?
4 Is the singer religious?

3 Writing and speaking

a The song is melancholic. In pairs, rewrite the song and make it positive by replacing key words.

All the trees are green
And the sky is blue …

b In groups, read your songs to each other. Which song seems the most positive?

c When people live a long way from home it is easy to become homesick. Look at these pictures and talk to your partner about each picture. How much would you miss it if you were away from home, and why? Which three things or people would you miss the most?

Songsheet 3
Walking in Memphis

1 Speaking

a In pairs, look at these photographs. What do you know about Elvis Presley?

b Now decide if these statements are True (T), or False (F).

1 Elvis Presley was a twin.   T ◯   F ◯
2 He was born in Memphis.   T ◯   F ◯
3 His most famous home was called "Graceland."   T ◯   F ◯
4 One of his most famous songs was "Green Suede Shoes."   T ◯   F ◯
5 His wife's name was Priscilla.   T ◯   F ◯
6 He had two children, Michael and Lisa Marie.   T ◯   F ◯

2 Vocabulary work

Talk about the meaning of the words and phrases in the box and then write
them in the most appropriate column.

to board	tomb	gospel	Reverend	prayer	sing	"do a little number"
to touch down		first-class ticket		play piano	the blues	

Traveling	Religion	Music

3 Listening and reading

a Listen to the song and choose the correct answers.

1 He traveled by: **a)** bus. **b)** plane. **c)** car.

2 It was: **a)** sunny. **b)** raining. **c)** snowing.

3 He saw: **a)** Elvis. **b)** Michael Jackson. **c)** Puff Daddy.

4 He went to a: **a)** religious meeting. **b)** shopping mall. **c)** hotel.

5 He: **a)** sang. **b)** played guitar. **c)** played the piano.

b Now read the lyrics and check your answers to 3a.

Walking in Memphis

Put on my blue suede shoes
And I boarded the plane
Touched down in the land of the Delta Blues
In the middle of the pouring rain
W.C. Handy – won't you look down over me
Yeah, I got a first-class ticket
But I'm blue as a boy can be

When I'm walking in Memphis
Walking with my feet ten feet off Beale
Walking in Memphis
But do I really feel the way I feel

Saw the ghost of Elvis
On Union Avenue
Followed him up to the gates of Graceland
Then I watched him walk right through
Now security they did not see him
They just hovered round his tomb
But there's a pretty little thing waiting for the king
Down in the jungle room

When I'm walking in Memphis
I was walking with my feet ten feet off Beale
Walking in Memphis
But do I really feel the way I feel

They've got catfish on the table
They've got gospel in the air
And Reverend Green would be glad to see you
When you haven't got a prayer
But boy you've got a prayer in Memphis

Now Muriel plays piano
Every Friday at the Hollywood
And they brought me down to see her
And they asked me if I would
Do a little number
And I sang with all my might
And she said "Tell me are you a Christian child?"
And I said "Ma'am, I am tonight"

When I'm walking in Memphis
Walking with my feet ten feet off Beale
Walking in Memphis
But do I really feel the way I feel

Put on my blue suede shoes
And I boarded the plane
Touched down in the land of the Delta Blues
In the middle of the pouring rain
Touched down in the land of the Delta Blues
In the middle of the pouring rain

4 Speaking

Sometimes fans visit the private homes of music and movie stars to take photographs or souvenirs, like a stone from the driveway. In groups, answer the questions.

1 Are you a fan of any celebrity? Who and why?

2 Would you visit their home if you knew where it was? Why or why not?

3 If you saw someone famous would you ask for their autograph or take their photo?

4 What are the advantages and disadvantages of being famous?

Songsheet 4
Give me a little more time

1 Vocabulary work

Match the word or phrase on the left with the definition on the right.

1 to cope
2 to make up your mind
3 to let someone down
4 to convince
5 to be in two minds
6 to complicate

to make something difficult
to disappoint someone
to be unable to choose
to decide
to manage a difficult situation
to persuade successfully

2 Listening

a Look at the pictures and predict what the song will be about.

b **Listen to the song and choose the correct option for each statement.**

1 She is singing to: **a)** her friend. **b)** her lover. **c)** her brother.
2 She thinks he is: **a)** a good friend to her. **b)** a bad friend to her. **c)** indifferent to her.
3 She wants their relationship: **a)** to change. **b)** to start. **c)** to end.

c **Now listen again and match the sentence halves on the left with the correct ending in the second column.**

Give me a little more time

1 You tried your best to show me   **a** That you understand
2 Said if there were days I was lonely   **b** You wanted to be the man
3 You tried your best, convinced me   **c** That you really cared
4 And if I needed someone to hold on to   **d** Just call you – you'd be there

5 Then I knew   **e** inside for you
6 All the feelings that I had   **f** Though many times I tried
7 I could not deny   **g** it was true

Chorus (x 2)
8 Give me a little more time   **h** Feelings getting stronger
9 'Cos you know I'm in two minds   **i** I need to make up my mind
10 Ooh, I just can't pretend any longer   **j** I wanna be more than your friend

11 You've been there when I've needed   **k** Though friends we have been
12 I just don't know how I'd cope   **l** Or is it just me?
13 Feelings have grown between us   **m** You've never let me down
14 Don't you think it complicates things   **n** Without you being around

15 Then I knew   **o** it was true
16 All the feelings that you had   **p** Though many times I tried ooh – ooh
17 I could not deny   **q** I shared them too

Chorus (x 2)
18 Give me a little more time   **r** Feelings getting stronger
19 'Cos you know I'm in two minds   **s** I need to make up my mind
20 Ooh, I just can't pretend any longer   **t** I wanna be more than your friend

3 Speaking

In groups, discuss these questions.

1 Do you prefer going on holiday with one friend, a group of friends or with your family?
2 Can a friend ever care for you as much as your family?
3 What makes a good relationship?
4 Is it really possible for a friend to become "more than a friend"?
5 Do you know of anybody that was in this situation? What happened?

Songsheet 5
Ironic

1 Vocabulary work

Match the expressions in these sentences with the correct meanings from the box below.

1   A 1998 **Chardonnay** is ideal with this dish.
2   He has spent three years on **death row** since his conviction for murder.
3   He knows someone in the government and now he's got a million-dollar contract. **It figures**!
4   They tell you to arrive at the airport an hour before the flight, but I like to **play it safe** and get there at least two hours in advance.
5   The kids **sneaked up on** their dad as he was sleeping on the beach and covered him in sand!
6   The police **blew up** a car parked outside the President's home.
7   There's always **a traffic jam** on the road into the city in the morning.
8   You can't smoke in the office, but we are allowed a ten-minute cigarette **break** twice a day.

> a) a place where prisoners wait to be executed   b) get close without being noticed   c) exploded
> d) a type of wine   e) a lot of cars in a line   f) That's logical   g) time off work   h) be very careful

2 Speaking and listening

a   The night before his flight, a man had a dream of a plane crash, so he cancelled his flight and stayed at home. Only, a plane crashed into his house – how ironic! Work with your partners to think of ironic things that could happen in the situations in the table. Make notes in the first column.

b   Now listen to the song and fill in the second column.

	Our ideas	The song	How ironic?
A lottery			
A prisoner on death row			
A wedding day			
A flight			
A traffic jam			
Meeting the man of your dreams			

🎧 **c** Now complete the gaps in the song with suitable words. Listen to the song again and check your answers. Then compare your answers with a partner.

(**Ironic**)

An old man turned ninety-eight: He won the lottery and died the (1) .... day

It's a black (2) .... in your Chardonnay: It's a death row pardon two minutes too late

Isn't it ironic ... don't you think?

Chorus:

It's like rain on your wedding day: It's a free ride when you've already (3) ....

It's the good advice that you just didn't (4) ....: Who would've thought ... it figures

Mr. Play It Safe was (5) .... to fly: He packed his suitcase and kissed his kids good-bye

He waited his whole damn life to take that flight: And as the plane crashed down he thought

"Well, isn't this (6) ...." And isn't it ironic ... don't you think?

Repeat Chorus

Well life has a funny way of sneaking up on you

When you think everything's okay and everything's going right

And life has a funny way of (7) ....

You think everything's gone wrong and everything blows up

In your face

A traffic jam when you're already late

A no-smoking sign on your (8) .... break

It's like 10,000 (9) .... when all you need is a knife

It's meeting the man of my dreams

and then meeting his beautiful wife

And isn't it ironic ... don't you think?

A little too ironic ... and yeah I really do think ...

Repeat Chorus

Well life has a funny way of sneaking up on you

And life has a funny, funny way of (10) ....

3 Speaking

a Look at the table in exercise 2b. In groups, put the six events in order from the most to least ironic. Put number '1' in the box for the most ironic, number '2' for the second most ironic, etc.

b Now compare your answers with other groups.

c In your new groups discuss anything ironic that has happened to you at school, in work, on holiday, or in relationships. Decide who has the most ironic experience and share it with the rest of the class.

Songsheet 6
I will always love you

1 Vocabulary work

Bitter: *strong black coffee without any sugar has a bitter taste.*

The word *bitter* can also be used to describe feelings. Here are some typical English expressions. Together with your partner, try to give personal examples or examples from the news or history of the following.

1   a bitter argument
2   feeling bitter at the way you've been treated
3   a bitter disappointment
4   bittersweet memories

2 Speaking

a   Match these songs with the artist and the movie they come from.

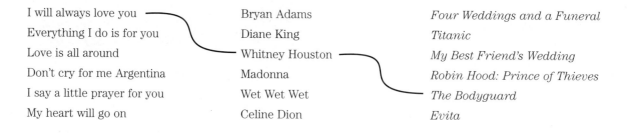

I will always love you	Bryan Adams	*Four Weddings and a Funeral*
Everything I do is for you	Diane King	*Titanic*
Love is all around	Whitney Houston	*My Best Friend's Wedding*
Don't cry for me Argentina	Madonna	*Robin Hood: Prince of Thieves*
I say a little prayer for you	Wet Wet Wet	*The Bodyguard*
My heart will go on	Celine Dion	*Evita*

b   Now see if you can agree on at least one example of the following.

1   *"Great song, but it's a shame about the movie."*

2   *"Great movie, but it's a shame about the song."*

3   *"Great song: great movie."*

4   *"I can't stand the song or the movie."*

3 Listening

a Listen to the song and answer these three questions.

1 Why does she think she should leave?

2 What will she take from the relationship?

3 How does she feel toward her partner?

b Now look at the words of the song and fill in the gaps. Then listen to the song again to check the answers.

I will always love you

If I should stay I would only be in your (1) ....

So I'll (2) .... but I (3) ....

I'll think of you every (4) .... of the way

And I will always love you

You, my (5) .... you, mmm

Bittersweet memories

That is (6) .... I'm taking with (7) ....

So, (8) .... , please don't (9) ....

We both know I'm not what you (10) ....

And I will always love you

I hope life (11) .... you kind

And I hope you have all you (12) .... of

And I wish you joy and (13) ....

But above all this I wish you (14) ....

And I will always love you

4 Speaking

Work in groups of three. Imagine that one of you is the character singing the song and that two of you are his / her best friends. One friend thinks you're crazy and should not leave. The other one thinks that leaving is the right thing to do. Begin the conversation by telling your friends:

"Listen, can I tell you something. I'm thinking about going away – on my own."

Continue the conversation with your two friends.

Irregular verbs

Infinitive	Past	Past participle	Unit and lesson
be	was / were	been	U1, L1
become	became	become	U2, L1
begin	began	begun	U3, L3
break	broke	broken	U4, L3
bring	brought	brought	Learning check 2
build	built	built	U2, L2
buy	bought	bought	U4, L1
can	could	–	U1, L2
catch	caught	caught	U5, L2
choose	chose	chosen	U3, L3
come	came	come	U1, L3
cost	cost	cost	U1, L2
deal	dealt	dealt	U2, L3
do	did	done	U1, L1
draw	drew	drawn	U2, L3
drink	drank	drunk	U5, L2
drive	drove	driven	U5, L4
eat	ate	eaten	U2, L4
fall	fell	fallen	Learning check 2
feel	felt	felt	U4, L2
find	found	found	U1, L1
fly	flew	flown	U5, L2
forget	forgot	forgotten	U12, L4
get	got	gotten	U1, L1
give	gave	given	U4, L2
go	went	gone	U1, L1
grow	grew	grown	U2, L3
have	had	had	U1, L1
hear	heard	heard	U2, L4
hit	hit	hit	U10, L2
keep	kept	kept	U1, L3
know	knew	known	U1, L2

Infinitive	Past	Past participle	Unit and lesson
leave	left	left	Learning check 3
lend	lent	lent	Learning check 5
let	let	let	U1, L3
lose	lost	lost	U2, L2
make	made	made	U1, L2
mean	meant	meant	U5, L1
meet	met	met	U4, L3
pay	paid	paid	U2, L4
put	put	put	U1, L3
read	read	read	U1, L1
run	ran	run	U10, L2
say	said	said	U5, L2
see	saw	seen	U6, L1
sell	sold	sold	U2, L3
send	sent	sent	U1, L2
show	showed	shown	U2, L3
sing	sang	sung	U7, L1
sink	sank	sunk	U5, L2
sit	sat	sat	U4, L3
speak	spoke	spoken	U1, L3
spend	spent	spent	U2, L2
steal	stole	stolen	U2, L2
take	took	taken	U2, L2
teach	taught	taught	U11, L3
tell	told	told	U1, L3
think	thought	thought	U1, L2
throw	threw	thrown	U4, L2
understand	understood	understood	U5, L1
wear	wore	worn	U5, L2
win	won	won	U2, L2
write	wrote	written	U1, L1

Pronunciation chart

Vowels

/i/	eat
/ɪ/	sit
/eɪ/	wait
/e/	get
/æ/	hat
/aɪ/	write
/ʌ/	but
/u:/	food
/ʊ/	good
/oʊ/	go
/ɔ:/	saw
/a/	hot
/aʊ/	cow
/ɔɪ/	boy
/iər/	here
/ər/	her
/eər/	hair
/or/	or
/ar/	far

Consonants
(shown as initial sounds)

/b/	bat
/k/	cat
/tʃ/	chair
/d/	dog
/f/	fat
/g/	girl
/h/	hat
/dʒ/	July
/k/	coat
/l/	like
/m/	man
/n/	new
/p/	pet
/kw/	queen
/r/	run
/s/	see
/ʃ/	shirt
/t/	talk
/ð/	the
/θ/	thin
/v/	voice
/w/	where
/j/	you
/ŋ/	sing (as final sound)
/z/	zoo

The alphabet

/eɪ/	/i/	/e/	/aɪ/	/oʊ/	/u:/	/ar/
Aa	Bb	Ff	Ii	Oo	Qq	Rr
Hh	Cc	Ll	Yy		Uu	
Jj	Dd	Mm			Ww	
Kk	Ee	Nn				
	Gg	Ss				
	Pp	Xx				
	Tt					
	Vv					
	Zz					

Macmillan Education
Between Towns Road, Oxford OX4 3PP
A division of Macmillan Publishers Limited
Companies and representatives throughout the world

ISBN 978 0 333 92753 3

Text © Simon Brewster, Paul Davies, Mickey Rogers 2002
Songsheets written by Martin McMorrow and Kate Fuscoe.
Design and illustration © Macmillan Publishers Limited 2002

First published 2002

Design, editorial and picture research by
Lodestone Publishing Limited (design: Mind's Eye Design)
Illustrated by Kathy Baxendale, Fred Van Deelen, Celia Hart,
Sue Potter, Andy Warrington, Geoff Waterhouse
Cover design by Katie Austin
Cover photo by Stone

Among all the people who contributed to the Skyline project, the
authors give special thanks to John Waterman and Lucy Torres, who
did much more than their duty as editors. Thank you, John and Lucy!
The authors would also like to thank Katie Austin for the cover design.

The publishers would like to thank the following for reading
material and making comments on books four and/or five: Maria
Luiza de Angeli, ESL Teacher, Development of special materials,
Colegio Santo Americo, São Paulo, Brazil; Vládia María Cabral
Borges, Professor of English Linguistics and Applied Linguistics,
Head of Department of Foreign Languages, University of Ceará,
Forteleza, Brazil; Lueli Loivos Ceruti, Director of Studies, RLC
Schools, Brazil; Heriberto Diaz, Head of the Language Department,
Centro de Investigación y Docencia Económicas, Mexico; Norma
Duarte Martinez, English Coordinator, Veterinary Medicine and
Husbandry College, National Autonomous University of Mexico,
Mexico D.F. Mexico; Albina Escobar, Freelance Teacher Trainer
and Consultant, Brazil; Consuelo F. B. Ivo, Supervisor, Centro
Cultural Brasil Estados Unidos Campinas, Brazil; Connie R.
Johnson, Co-ordinator of EFL Basic 1 and EFL Professor in the
Language Department, Universidad de las Américas Puebla,
México; Carlos Meléndez, Tecnologico de Monterrey Campus
Guadalajara, Mexico; JoAnn Miller, English Language Academic
Coordinator, Universidad del Valle de México, A.C., Mexico; Joacyr
T. Oliveira, Executive Coordinator, União Cultural Brasil Estados
Unidos, São Paulo, Brazil; Jorge Adolfo Obregon Aragon, English
Coordinator, Instituto Chapultepec A.C., Culiacan, Mexico; Ane
Cibele Palma, Academic Coordinator, Centro Cultural Brasil
Estados Unidos Curitiba, Inter Americano-Curitiba, Brazil; Kathryn
Laura Sagert, English teacher, Centro de Investigación y Docencia
Económicas, Mexico.

The authors and publishers gratefully acknowledge the following for
permission to reproduce copyright material. Every effort has been
made to trace copyright holders, but in some cases this has proved
impossible. The publishers would be happy to hear from any
copyright holder that has not been acknowledged.

Adapted extract from Amazon.Com Book Review 'The Mozart Effect'
from www.arkanar.minsk.by/118/Mozart_Effect.htm, reprinted by
permission of the publisher; Adapted extract from 'One
Thousaaaaahhhhh… Shit' by David Banks, from Parachuting with
Barry from www.pyteeoh.demon.uk/extreme/parachut.htm reprinted
by permission of the author; Adapted extract from 'Barbie's Girl

Power' by Jessica Callan from The Electronic Telegraph 28.01.99,
copyright © Telegraph Group Limited 1999, reprinted by permission of
the publishers; California Dreamin' words and music by John Phillips
and Michelle Phillips © 1965 Wingate Music Corporation, USA.
Universal/MCA Music Limited, 77 Fulham Palace Road, London, W6,
reprinted by permission of Music Sales Ltd. All Rights Reserved.
International Copyright Secured; Give Me a Little More Time words
and music by Gabrielle, Andy Dean, Benjamin Wolff & Ben Barson,
© 1995 EMI Music Publishing Ltd/Polygram Music Publishing Ltd &
Perfect Songs Ltd, London, WC2H 0QY & Universal Music Limited,
77 Fulham Palace Road, London, W6, reprinted by permission of
EMI Music Publishing Ltd, IMP Ltd and Music Sales Ltd. All Rights
Reserved. International Copyright Secured; I Will Always Love You
words and music by Dolly Parton © 1973 Velvet Apple Music, reprinted
by permission of Carlin Music Corp, London, NW1 8BD.
All Rights Reserved; Ironic words by Alanis Morissette music by Alanis
Morissette & Glen Ballard © 1995 Music Corporation of America
Incorporated, Vanhurst Place, MCA Music Publishing & Aerostation
Corporation, USA. Universal/MCA Music Ltd, 77 Fulham Palace Road,
London W6, reprinted by permission of Music Sales Ltd. All Rights
Reserved. International Copyright Secured; Oops!... I Did it Again
Words and Music by Max Martin and Rami © 2000 Zomba Music
Publishers Limited, 165 –167 High Road, London, NW10 2SG,
reproduced by permission of Music Sales Ltd. All Rights Reserved.
International Copyright Secured. Tears in Heaven words and music by
Eric Clapton & Will Jennings © 1992 & 1995 E.C. Music Limited,
London, NW1 and Blue Sky Rider Songs, reprinted by permission of
Music Sales Limited and Hal Leonard Corporation. All Rights
Reserved. International Copyright Secured; The Logical Song
Hodgson/Davies © 1979, reprinted by permission of Universal Music
Publishing Ltd; Walking in Memphis words and music by Marc Cohn ©
1991 Museum Steps Music and W B Music Corp, USA Warner/
Chappell Music Ltd, London W6 8BS, reprinted by permission of IMP
Ltd. All rights reserved.

The author and publishers would like to thank the following for
permission to reproduce their photographs; AKG pp42(t), 44(br),
66A(Lessing), 66E(Binder); AP pp19(E), 19(F)(Maakjterrill), 46, 52,
66C(Djansezian), 86(r), 90(t), 109(Yu); John Birdsall p10A; Bridgeman
Art Library p43(l)(© ADAGP, Paris and DACS, London 2002), 43(r)(©
ADAGP, Paris and DACS, London 2002); Bubbles p68(Woodcock);
Corbis pp42(b), 72D(Thompson), 86(c)(Bettman), 87, 88(Rowell),
90(b); Eye Ubiquitous pp10E(Skjold), 19(C)(Grau), 32(C)(Fairclough),
34(Hawkins), 72C(Wilson), 98A(Skjold); Genesis/NASA p116; James
Davis Worldwide pp32(B), 125, 111(G,H); Kobal pp19(D)(20th Century
Fox/Paramount), 51(Rank), 104(b)(MGM/United Artists),
105(MGM/United Artists), 118(B); Mary Evans Picture Library p44(bl);
Moviestore p104(t)(MGM/United Artists); PA Photos pp18(tl),
19(A)(EPA), 61(l)(EPA), 61(r)(Melville), 66D(Abaca), 106(l), 107(r);
Popperfoto pp54(Reuters/Behrakis), 63(Reuters/Braley), 86(l), 118(A);
Powerstock/Zefa pp9, 10B, 14(tl), 19(B), 32(C), 37(Enticknap), 38, 55,
80(tr), 81(l,r), 84, 96(tr), 98B, 111(B,C,D,E); Redferns p66B(Hutson),
114(Hutson), 118(C)(Michael Ochs Archive); Rex Features
pp48(Weus), 66F(Adebari), 79(Sipa), 121(Meddle); Stock Directory
(TCL) p80(b)(Mo); Sylvia Cordaïy pp96(tl)(Whiting), 111(A);
Telegraph Colour Library pp7(Krasowitz), 10C(Fruchet), 10D(Gelot),
14(tr)(Traza), 44(t)(Adams), 66(l)(Hippisley), 69(Childs),
70(r)(Tilley), 72A(Scott), 106/7(Simpson), 111(F)(Croucher); Tografox
pp6(A,B), 70(l), 96(br), 100(Williams); Travel Ink pp18(tr)(Enoch),
72B(Badkin); John Walmesley pp80(tl), 98(C,D).
Commissioned photographs by Robert Battersby pp6(C), 62, 64, 78,
96(bl); Nick Webster p60.

Printed in Thailand.

2012 2011 2010 2009 2008
14   13   12   11   10